MARYLAND FREEDOM SEEKERS
on the
UNDERGROUND RAILROAD

JENNY MASUR

FOREWORD BY CHERYL JANIFER LAROCHE
INTRODUCTION BY MAYA D. DAVIS

THE
History
PRESS

Published by The History Press
Charleston, SC
www.historypress.com

First published 2023

Manufactured in the United States

ISBN 9781467148719

Library of Congress Control Number: 2022944974

Notice: The information in this book is true and complete to the best of our knowledge. It is offered without guarantee on the part of the author or The History Press. The author and The History Press disclaim all liability in connection with the use of this book.

To those who work to uncover and share the history of Maryland's freedom seekers

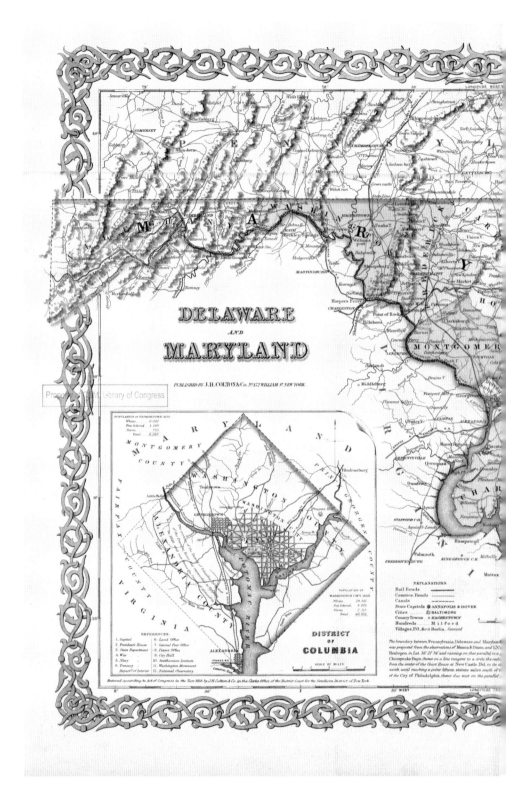

DELAWARE
AND
MARYLAND

PUBLISHED BY J.H. COLTON & Co. N° 172 WILLIAM S.T. NEW YORK.

POPULATION OF GEORGETOWN 1850.
White 6.081
Free Colored . 1.560
Slaves 725
Total 8.366

POPULATION OF
WASHINGTON CITY 1850.
White 29.945
Free Colored . 8.075
Slaves 2.113
Total .. 40.001

DISTRICT
OF
COLUMBIA

SCALE OF MILES

REFERENCES.
1. Capitol
2. Presidents House
3. State Department
4. War
5. Navy
6. Treasury
   Depart.t of Interior
7. Land Office
8. General Post Office
9. Patent Office
10. Smithsonian Institute
11. Washington Monument
12. National Observatory

Entered according to Act of Congress in the Year 1855 by J.H. Colton & Co. in the Clerks Office of the District Court for the Southern District of New York

EXPLANATIONS
Rail Roads
Common Roads
Canals
State Capitals ⊛ ANNAPOLIS ⊛ DOVER
Cities .... ☰ BALTIMORE
County Towns .. ∘ HAGERSTOWN
Hundreds .... Milford
Villages, P.O. &c ∘ Berlin, Gosport

G3830 1855 .C6

Nº22.

This J. Colton map from 1855 shows Maryland in relation to Delaware and Pennsylvania. *Library of Congress.*

CONTENTS

CONTENTS

FOREWORD

I f the first half of the twentieth century can be considered the low point of Underground Railroad studies, then the first half of the twenty-first century has seen its resurrection. Early works by Larry Gara (1961), Charles Blockson (1987) and John Hope Franklin and Loren Schweninger (1999) laid out new themes. As Larry Gara stressed in his influential work *The Liberty Line*, African Americans were central in the cause of their own liberation. Charles Blockson, in his several books and articles on the Underground Railroad, brought the involvement of the Black church, Black communities and fraternal organizations into sharp focus.

Maryland Freedom Seekers on the Underground Railroad continues and extends these directions. Its meticulous assembling of new evidence, naming of obscured activists and making connections across states and nations contribute to this expansive era. Increasingly, as we better understand the inner workings of the Underground Railroad, works such as Masur's fit together more pieces of the puzzle. A clearer picture is emerging from dozens of new books.

With escapes from Maryland as the starting point, Masur presents fresh stories from a variety of lesser-known examples. The freedom seekers and their determination to free themselves from slavery are at the center of the action. Broken promises, betrayal and legal wrangling, seizure and arrest marked their journeys out of slavery. Trepidation, anticipation, apprehension and determination drove their successful journeys toward freedom. Kidnappers, slave catchers and re-enslavement, particularly after

1850, were an ever-present threat. Moving through a thicket of assumed names and hasty sanctuaries, relocations, confrontations and rescues, Masur exposes the multiple strategies for claiming and maintaining that hard-won freedom.

We see the Underground Railroad as the complex and dangerous undertaking that it was. The harrowing struggle of getting oneself out of slavery once arrest and fugitive slave laws took effect lays bare the legal consequences and inner workings of the Underground Railroad. *Maryland Freedom Seekers* deftly uses slave narratives, court cases and fragments of known stories to look across the arc of freedom seekers' lives, often following them to the end of their days.

Maryland's location, with its long northern border with Pennsylvania and proximity to Philadelphia, ensured that the state experienced a record number of escapes from slavery. Yet, four or five narratives—those of Frederick Douglass, Harriet Tubman, Josiah Henson and J.W.C. Pennington, for example—have dominated Maryland's Underground Railroad stories. Added to these, the Maryland escapes that saturate William Still's famous work *The Underground Railroad* helped push lesser-known escapes to the margins. Emphasis on escape routes over people also contributed to the silencing of the Underground Railroad's main actors.

By emphasizing different moments in the escape narratives, Masur manages to contribute different stories while covering most of the major escape strategies of the Underground Railroad and a few lesser ones, as well. Unnoticed escapes during routine weekend visits to family or over long weekends and holidays gave freedom seekers such as Moses Viney or Nathan Mead, also known as Alexander Hemsley, a head start. They timed their escapes in order to gain several days before escape advertisements could be placed in local newspapers. From waterborne escapes on whaling vessels to major rescues by Black community members, the stories push into underexplored territory. John Thompson went to sea on a New Bedford whaler and found the ocean to be the ultimate refuge.

The role of the Black church as a site of sanctuary and assistance to freedom seekers becomes increasingly visible with new studies and stories. In my own work, the Black church, particularly the African Methodist Episcopal (AME) Church alongside the AME Zion and Black Baptists, has shaped my understanding of how African Americans helped one another in their journeys toward freedom. Methodist camp meetings as one pathway out of slavery show up in the narratives. Some escapees were themselves ministers or were helped by ministers.

The experiences of women, enslaved and free, both broaden and deepen our understanding of their important contributions. Once they embraced their freedom, women were both the rescuers and the rescued, proactive, insistent and forceful. In the case of Matilda Neal, she initiated and engineered her own escape without the help or assistance of her free husband, Richard. The couple's story represents numerous untold escape stories of women and their families. But even in these lesser-known stories, the mainstays of the Underground Railroad appear again and again. The Reverends Charles B. Ray and Theodore S. Wright are familiar accomplices. The involvement of Lewis Tappan and Quaker activists still strikes a familiar chord.

I have often noticed, with a level of frustration, in my own research the casual mention that a freedom seeker was born in Maryland. This information was almost always noted in passing or gleaned from census data gathered for a different purpose. Freedom seekers' Maryland origins rarely seemed to lead to new revelations, probably because they were on their way out of state to somewhere else—anywhere other than Maryland. Here, however, between these pages, we read about a range of Maryland escapes. We understand their sufferings, triumphs and defeats as Masur follows them out of slavery but into a tenuous freedom across varying geographies.

Maryland Freedom Seekers has benefitted from the National Park Service's National Underground Railroad Network to Freedom, a cooperative program with a collaborative approach. The program relies on people across the country contributing their local knowledge and expertise to uncover the Underground Railroad network of stories. This book emerges out of that tradition.

At this point, I have read more than my share of Underground Railroad narratives and glimpsed fragments of escapes through hundreds, maybe thousands, of escape advertisements. In many ways, however, I think the work of uncovering new dimensions of Underground Railroad stories is in its infancy. There are many more known stories that need attention and new stories waiting to be discovered or proven. What Masur has provided is a human adventure. She shows us how these stories fit together, how they connect across time and space, across communities and people. We do not have to wonder, "What happened to them?"

Cheryl Janifer LaRoche, PhD
Kensington, Maryland
March 2022

PREFACE

My interest in the Underground Railroad comes thanks to the National Park Service. I worked with the National Park Service for twenty-five years, of which seventeen were with the National Underground Railroad Network to Freedom, a program mandated by Congress in 1998. In 2015, I retired from the government but found I was unable to retire from investigating and publicizing the history of the Underground Railroad. I decided to write this book.

If the Underground Railroad is defined as "resistance to slavery through flight," that includes a broader meaning, a wider geography and a longer history than restricting it to antebellum organized networks. It is not coincidental that this book does not focus on the organized networks of the Underground Railroad that have been widely studied, written about and adapted to film. The definition of the "Underground Railroad" typically does not make those escaping central to the narrative. It refers primarily to abolitionists from northern states who successfully aided the escape of formerly enslaved people. The latter narrative is sometimes true but only accounts for a small percentage of incidents. Many anonymous or lesser-known individuals across the United States put their lives on the line, for varying motives, in order that those fleeing slavery could find freedom. Those assisting the people fleeing were antislavery but not necessarily politically active.

This book focuses on self-liberating African Americans, whom I will call "freedom seekers." Self-liberators may have been a small percentage of those in slavery, but they were significant in that their escapes created alarm in slaveholders and hope for others still enslaved. "Freedom seeker" is used to avoid other more derogatory terms. "Fugitive" and "runaway" legitimize the possibility of one human being owning title to another. Similarly, before their escapes, I will refer to freedom seekers either as "enslaved," because slavery was an imposed and impermanent condition, or as "bondsmen," because bondage in slavery was mandated by law before the Civil War.

I chose to restrict the subjects of the book to Maryland because Maryland is lucky to have a partnership among the Maryland Office of Tourism, the Maryland State Archives and the National Underground Railroad Network to Freedom. Together, they document and publicize resistance to slavery through flight. The state archives has created an excellent "Legacy of Slavery in Maryland" website with profiles of freedom seekers from almost all the state's counties and a database of hundreds of documents. Using National Underground Railroad Network to Freedom designations, the Maryland Office of Tourism has produced a listing of Underground Railroad sites and educational programs that also includes libraries and archives equipped with resources to facilitate Underground Railroad research (see the appendix).

The faces of flight in Maryland are well-known figures, such as Frederick Douglass and Harriet Tubman. The majority of documented Maryland freedom seekers are unknown to the general public. Every Maryland county has stories of flight from or through it, whether or not the stories have been investigated or publicly acknowledged.

In picking subjects for the book, I sought variety in the lives on which I chose to focus. Within those lives, I sought emphases on different moments—slavery, escape and maturity. As many counties as possible were covered. I included women and children as well as men and people with varying motivations and destinations.

Whenever possible, I wanted to look at the internal changes accompanying attainment of liberty. From the time of their escapes, the self-liberators underwent emotional, intellectual and spiritual transformations that continued until they died. They were forced to remake themselves. They had to adapt to the drawbacks as well as the benefits of their new lives.

I looked for individuals about whom there was sufficient material, whether researched directly by me and/or by local historians who were willing to share. I avoided well-known figures or those undergoing research by someone already planning to publish.

I call the content of the chapters "stories," but they are historical accounts. They are documented by primary sources—that is, credible period documents created by those present at the events described or those alive at the time with access to firsthand accounts. For all nine chapters, whenever possible, I found other types of sources, like censuses or estate inventories, to corroborate the main primary sources. Thus, I had to exclude one exciting narrative by a gold rush participant, because I could not confirm enough details. I attempted to support my statements and opinions and to give credit to other historians. Although there are no footnotes in this book, the draft had 688. Interpretation of sources is mine, dependent on my own perspectives and biases.

There is much mystery about the experiences of enslaved people in Maryland prior to escaping, because most documentation comes from the time after freedom seekers left Maryland. I was lucky enough to find nine subjects with sufficiently detailed origins. Three authors of slave narratives—Isaac Mason, John Thompson and James Watkins—discussed their time in, and escapes from, Maryland. When interviewed by Benjamin Drew, Reverend Alexander Helmsley likewise described his life in Maryland and his flight. A descendant of the former owner of Richard Neal inherited family papers replete with documentation on Richard and his wife, Matilda. Several of the freedom seekers—Basil Dorsey, Reverend Alexander Helmsley and James Hamlet, as well as Hester Norman's husband, George, were involved in legal proceedings from which records or transcriptions have survived.

By concentrating on a few individuals from Maryland, I aim to replace stereotypes with human beings. Underground Railroad participants felt human yearnings, fear, enduring love, altruism and determination. In particular, those escaping slavery deserve to be celebrated for their resilience, courage, resolve and resourcefulness. Their upbringing in slavery is no excuse to overlook their intelligence, persistence, strength of character or shrewdness in assessment of whom to trust.

The aim of this book is to educate and inspire the public. There is great interest in the Underground Railroad, although at the same time, there are many stereotypes and misconceptions. May this book stimulate further research on the freedom seekers you will get to know and on others still unknown.

By writing this book, I hope to make a contribution toward healing racial wounds and misunderstanding. We can be proud of the heroes described in this book for their accomplishments despite the worst of circumstances. They are an inspiration today as we combat discrimination and racism.

Jenny Masur
Washington, D.C.
March 2022

ACKNOWLEDGEMENTS

First, I thank The History Press and my editor, Kate Jenkins, who enabled me to tell these stories.

I cannot leave out those at the National Park Service who taught me over seventeen years about the Underground Railroad—the members of the team of the National Underground Railroad Network to Freedom Program headed by Diane Miller.

The introduction by Maya D. Davis would have been impossible without Chris Haley, Maryland State Archives; David Armenti, Maryland Center for History and Culture; Heather Ersts, Maryland State Tourism; and Celeste Bernier, University of Edinburgh.

A pandemic makes doing research difficult. I have often depended on the kindness of colleagues. Fellow historians, librarians, archivists, staff at historical societies and preservation planners in many places shared their expertise with me, whether from a distance or in person. If I have left someone out, I apologize.

Historians specializing in local history like Emilie Amt, Tom Calarco, Chris Densmore, Dean Herrin, Lucy Maddox, Tony Morris, Steve Strimer, Neil Yetwin, Joan Szablewski and Cooper Wingert shared their expertise, favorite heroes and research with me and often helped with editing and fact-checking. Many colleagues and friends suggested subjects for chapters. Although I did not end up including the freedom seekers for whom they provided sources, I owe a debt to Richard Elia, Jody Fernald, Pat Guida, Deanda Johnson, Robin Kravitz, Don Papson and staff at the Uxbridge

Free Public Library. I became acquainted with two of the book's heroes through applications to the National Underground Railroad Network to Freedom relating to Moses Viney and Basil Dorsey.

Donna DiPaolo, Marian Eaton, Eva Slezak and Pat Vondal were among the friends and colleagues who helped me edit and check the chapters for accuracy and clarity. Pat Vondal, Molly Clark, Corinne Masur and Sandy Schmidt offered hospitality and opportunities for research. My family provided encouragement and support. Margie Ware stands above all for her help, especially providing transportation and faithful companionship.

Abroad, in Canada, I am grateful to Helen Booth at St. Catharines Museum & Welland Canal Centre, Rochelle Bush at St. Catharines Historical Society and the librarian at St. Catharines Public Library. In Great Britain, I am indebted to Hannah-Rose Murray, the Manchester and Lancashire Family History Society and the Worcestershire County Council.

In the United States, I have many debts scattered across the landscape. In Connecticut, I should thank the Historical Preservation Planner, State Library, Farmington Historical Society and Maureen Heher, Hartford History Center, Hartford Public Library. Massachusetts was the destination of two chapters' heroes, so I am grateful to people in New Bedford, Northampton and Worcester. They include: in Worcester, Janette Thomas Greenwood of Clark University, Wendy Essery and Madeline Ryan of Worcester Historical Museum and staff at the Worcester Public Library; in Florence, the David Ruggles Center; in the Black River Valley, Chuck Arning, park ranger extraordinaire; in New Bedford, staff at the New Bedford History Room of the New Bedford Public Library and Mark Procknik at the New Bedford Whaling Museum. In New York, I appreciated help in Schenectady from Marlaine DesChamps and Jim Gerencser, archive specialists, Union College; novelist Gretchel Hathaway; Marietta Carr at Schenectady County Historical Society; and staff at Schenectady Public Library. Adrienne Lang at the Brooklyn Historical Society, like the others, went out of her way to be helpful. In New Jersey, when tracking Alexander Helmsley in Burlington County, I turned to the local park system, the public library, the courthouse and the Prison Museum Association in Mount Holly; Vivian Thiele at the New Jersey State Archives; and Regina Fitzpatrick at the New Jersey State Library. Many freedom seekers traveled through Pennsylvania, so I appreciated the following help: in Cumberland County, Cara Curtis at Cumberland County Historical Society and the county archivist Barbara Bartos; John A. Miller, Shippensburg Historical Society; and in Carlisle itself, Matt Pinsker, History Department, and Jim

Gerencser, college archivist, Dickinson College; in Bucks County, Annie Halliday, library and archives manager at the Mercer Museum and Library of Bucks County Historical Society and Pat Witek, Doylestown Historical Society; and in Philadelphia, Erica Harman and staff at the Eastern State Penitentiary Historic Site.

Finally, of course, I had to research the freedom seekers' origins, and so across Maryland I thank Anne Kyle, Maryland State Tourism; Chris Haley, Megan Craynon and Maria Day, Maryland State Archives; in Baltimore, Eva Slezak, Enoch Pratt Free Library; on the Eastern Shore, Monique Gordy of Talbot County Maryland Room, Joan Andersen of Kent County Historical Society, John Schratwieser of Kent Cultural Alliance, Patricia Clark of Kent County Public Library and historians Carol and Alex M. Wilson, Washington College; and in Frederick County, Amanda Whitmore, historic preservation planner. In Hagerstown, I thank Elizabeth Howe, Western Maryland Room of Hagerstown Public Library; Brett Peters at Washington County Historical Society; Stephen Bockmiller, the Hagerstown city planner. Finally, I thank longtime Baltimore County historian John McGrain, may he rest in peace.

Despite all this help, I claim all errors as my own.

CHRONOLOGY

Boldface entries refer to persons or events relevant to this book. *Italicized* entries name events relevant to Maryland.

1634	*Settlers who founded the colony of Maryland in St. Mary's City included Mathias de Sousa (African descent), an indentured servant*
1663–64	*Maryland legalized slavery*
1664	*Thomas Cornwalleys of St. Mary's County purchased the first two bondsmen in Maryland*
1763–68	Mason-Dixon line surveyed
1775	Pennsylvania Abolition Society established
	Dunmore's Proclamation promised British freedom to rebellious enslaved African Americans in the Chesapeake
1780	Pennsylvania's Gradual Abolition Act
1783	Massachusetts Supreme Court abolished slavery
1784	Connecticut's Gradual Emancipation Act
	Maryland prohibited importation of enslaved African Americans

1786	*First freedom suits in Maryland*
1789	United States Constitution
1791–1804	Haitian Revolution
1793	Fugitive Slave Act
1794	Cotton gin patented Mother Bethel African Methodist Episcopal Church established in Philadelphia by Reverend Richard Allen
1796	*Maryland Manumission Laws liberalized*
1799	New York's Gradual Emancipation Law
1804	New Jersey passed a gradual abolition act
1808	United States banned international slave trade
1812–15	War of 1812
1816–17	American Colonization Society created
1820	Missouri Compromise
1826	Pennsylvania's first personal liberty law
1829	David Walker's *Appeal* published
1820s	**Nathan Mead (ALEXANDER HELMSLEY) ran from Isaac Baggs**
1827	*James W.C. Pennington ran from Washington County* Total abolition of slavery in New York
1831	Nat Turner Revolt William Lloyd Garrison established *The Liberator*

1832	*Maryland responded to Nat Turner Revolt with new restrictions on African Americans*
1833	American Anti-Slavery Society founded
1834	Slavery Abolition Act took effect in the British Empire New York Vigilance Committee organized
1835	**JOHN THOMPSON ran from James Wagar**
1836	**Ephraim Costly (BASIL DORSEY) ran from Thomas Sollers** **Helmsley Trial in New Jersey** **Helmsley and family fled to Canada**
1837	**Basil Dorsey trial in Doylestown**
1837–52	Philadelphia Vigilant Committee
1838	*Frederick Douglass escaped from Baltimore*
1840	**Perry Thomas (MOSES VINEY) ran from Richard Murphy** New York's second personal liberty law
1841	Amistad Supreme Court decision
1842	*Prigg v. Pennsylvania* Supreme Court decision
1842–44	**John Thompson worked as steward on whaler**
1843	Massachusetts personal liberty law
1844	**Sam Berry (JAMES WATKINS) ran from Luke Ensor** **Basil Dorsey and family arrived in Bensonville (Florence)**
1845	Narrative of the Life of Frederick Douglass *published* *Frederick Douglass found refuge in Britain* **James Watkins arrived in Hartford**

1846   **Bill Thompson (ISAAC MASON) ran from James Mansfield, Jr.**

1847   **Moses Viney hired by President Eliphalet Nott, Union College**
HESTER NORMAN ran from James Kennedy
Rescue of Ann Brown and Hester Norman (McClintock Riot)
Pennsylvania personal liberty law
North Star *published by Frederick Douglass*

1848   **JAMES HAMLET ran from Mary Brown**
Thomas Garrett convicted for helping freedom seekers in Delaware

1849   **MATILDA NEAL ran from Isaac Mayo**
Harriet Tubman ran from Dorchester County

1850   Fugitive Slave Act (September) as part of Compromise of 1850
James Hamlet caught and, after mass meetings, redeemed by community (October)
Moses Viney ran to Canada
Anthony Burns returned to Virginia
Isaac Mason ran to Canada

1851   **James Watkins sailed to England**
Community redeemed freedom of Basil Dorsey
Austin Williams arranged freedom of James Watkins
Christiana Resistance in response to pursuit by Maryland owner Edward Gorsuch
Rachel Parker kidnapping

1852   ***Narrative of the Life of James Watkins* published**
Moses Viney returned from Canada to Schenectady
Uncle Tom's Cabin became a best-seller

1853　　**Richard Neal abducted by Isaac Mayo**
　　　　Twelve Years a Slave published by Solomon Northup

1854　　**James Watkins brought family to England**
　　　　Kansas-Nebraska Act

1855　　Massachusetts Personal Liberty Act
　　　　Alexander Helmsley died

1856　　Benjamin Drew published *A North-Side View of Slavery*
　　　　Bleeding Kansas began
　　　　The Life of John Thompson, a Fugitive Slave
　　　　published

1857　　Dred Scott Supreme Court decision

1859　　John Brown's Raid
　　　　John Thompson died

1860　　**Isaac Mason sailed to Haiti**
　　　　Abraham Lincoln elected president

1861　　Attack on Fort Sumter

1862　　District of Columbia Emancipation Act

1863　　Emancipation Proclamation signed
　　　　Beginning of recruitment and enlistment of 200,000
　　　　　　African Americans in Union army and navy

1864　　Fugitive Slave Act repealed
　　　　Maryland constitution changed to abolish slavery

1865　　Thirteenth Amendment ratified
　　　　Ku Klux Klan founded

1866	**Moses Viney returned to Maryland and adopted his sister Leila**
	Isaac Mason returned to Maryland with Reverend George Offley's mission
1868	Fourteenth Amendment ratified
1870	Fifteenth Amendment ratified
1872	**Basil Dorsey died**
1875	Civil Rights Act
1876	Rutherford B. Hayes elected
	Withdrawal of federal troops from Louisiana and South Carolina, signaling end of Reconstruction
1881	**Richard Neal died**
1883	Parts of 1875 Civil Rights Act ruled unconstitutional
1890s–1920s	Peak of lynchings
1893	*Life of Isaac Mason as a Slave* published
1896	*Plessy v. Ferguson* Supreme Court decision
1898	**Isaac Mason died**
1909	**Moses Viney died**

FLIGHT FROM SLAVERY IN MARYLAND TO FREEDOM

Maryland is a state particularly useful for studying escapes on the Underground Railroad. It has thousands of documented incidents of daring escape attempts, permanent or otherwise, from its colonial period through emancipation. Maryland's rate of successful escapes is perhaps higher than any other state's except Kentucky and Virginia. Out of slavery in Maryland came such accomplished and distinguished individuals as Harriet Tubman, Frederick Douglass, Henry Highland Garnet, James W.C. Pennington and Samuel Ringgold Ward.

The colony of Maryland was founded in 1632, with its first settlers arriving in 1634. Maryland's geographic makeup includes a western mountain region, the southern plains, the piedmont plateau and part of the Chesapeake Bay's Eastern Shore. Vast differences in these regions showcase the varied experiences in slave escapes. Formative in Maryland's development were the Chesapeake Bay, which divides it in half, and the Potomac River, which divides it from Virginia. Many Marylanders were watermen accustomed to navigating its waterways, a skill useful for escape.

Maryland has a long, complicated history of the enslavement of Black people. The first man of African descent to arrive in Maryland was Mathias de Sousa, who entered the colony in 1634 as an indentured servant, not as a bondsman. Maryland did not legalize slavery until Maryland planters began importing more and more Africans to enslave as cheap labor for their new cash crop, tobacco. To legitimize their slavery, in 1664, Maryland passed a law equating race with enslavement and making the enslaved condition

Left: Elisa Greenwell, woman of mystery, escaped from the residence of William Edelen of Leonardtown, St. Mary's County, in 1859. *Collection of the Smithsonian National Museum of African American History and Culture.*

Below: The United Nations Educational, Scientific and Cultural Organization identified Annapolis as a documented entry point for Africans brought for enslavement. *VisitAnnapolis.org.*

hereditary. The United Nations Educational, Scientific and Cultural Organization has identified Annapolis, Baltimore and Oxford as documented entry points for Africans coming into Maryland. By the eighteenth century, slavery existed in every corner of the state but was concentrated most heavily in the lower Western Shore.

Slavery in Maryland differed from slavery farther south. Holdings of land and groupings of enslaved populations tended to be smaller. Most slaveholding families had small to mid-sized farms and maintained a workforce ranging from ten to twenty individuals. The few exceptions include those plantation communities owned by two state governors, Edward Lloyd and Charles Carnan Ridgely, with more than three hundred enslaved people tending to hundreds of acres of cash crops. As opposed to states situated in the Deep South, Maryland had the advantage of bordering the free state of Pennsylvania, which could serve as a conduit to liberty in other northern cities and states. By the nineteenth century, Maryland had a sizable free Black population ready to collude with fleeing bondsmen.

To offset these advantages, however, because its enslaved population had become self-perpetuating, Maryland had a domestic slave trade threatening the stability of enslaved African Americans. In the mid-nineteenth century, Maryland farmers shifted away from tobacco cultivation in favor of mixed agriculture, particularly grains. These crops did not demand the large enslaved workforce needed for intensive, year-round care. As cotton production increased in the Deep South, there was an increased demand for enslaved bodies to produce the crop. Entrepreneurs in the domestic slave trade took advantage of this change. Starting in the 1830s, companies like Franklin & Armfield of Alexandria, Virginia, sold slaves from Maryland and Virginia to southern states like Mississippi and Louisiana.

Rather than being less harsh than elsewhere, Maryland slavery also inflicted punishments, murders and rapes on African Americans. From its beginnings, the Maryland Colony faced resistance from enslaved Africans, forcibly removed from their respective kingdoms. Some enslaved people petitioned for freedom as early as the seventeenth century. Freedom petitions rose during the late eighteenth century, when enslaved individuals sued their owners for freedom on the basis of descent from White women. Petitions carried over into the nineteenth century, enabling liberation for many families, such as the Butlers, Mahoneys and Queens.

Slave escapes were another form of resistance as enslaved Africans and their descendants became more knowledgeable of the geography and landscape and built networks among friends and relatives across the region. Bondsmen moved when their owners relocated or married or when estates were divided among heirs living away from the home property. Enslaved coachmen, watermen, valets, market men and cooks traditionally accompanied their owners or had tasks that required they travel off-site. The formation of cross-plantation societies meant interaction with the enslaved people on other properties.

From the eighteenth century on, Maryland newspapers like the *Maryland Gazette* allowed owners to place advertisements with rewards to reclaim their escaped bondsmen. The advertisements included physical descriptions of the person who escaped and likely destinations. In addition, wealthier citizens also had broadside posters placed around the state. Governor Samuel Sprigg ordered one thousand copies of a broadside for two of his enslaved men, Clem and William Whittington, who escaped in 1815. The numbers of resisters through flight can only be estimated, due to multiple attempts, lack of reporting and lack of documentary evidence.

Maryland, like other southern states, saw an increase in slave escapes during the nineteenth century, as shown by the numbers of runaway advertisements, commitment notices, complaints in newspapers and local and statewide meetings of slaveholders. At a convention held in Annapolis in 1842 to protect the institution of slavery, slaveholders discussed influencing the legislature to pass more stringent laws. The slaveholders wanted prevention of all manumissions and of entry of free Negroes from other states and an increase in rewards for runaways.

Like other border states (Delaware, Kentucky, Missouri), Maryland was divided in its opinion about and practice of enslavement. The border states had smaller enslaved populations in comparison with the slaveholding states in the Deep South and were thought to be locations of neutrality during the Civil War. However, the internal division in the attitudes of the state's citizens, and even families, impacted the state's enslaved community.

In addition to its restrictive slave code applicable to anyone of African descent, as escapes became more prevalent, Maryland began enacting laws that limited the movement of the enslaved population. For example, in 1751, the general assembly enacted a law that

> *where any Slave shall be guilty of rambling, riding, going abroad in the Night, riding Horses in the Daytime without Leave, or running away, it shall be lawful for the Justices of the County Court, upon the application or complaint of the Master of such slave will immediately be punished by whipping, cropping, or branding in the cheek with the Letter R.*

To placate the South and reinforce a provision in the constitution, President George Washington signed into law the Fugitive Slave Act of 1793, which facilitated slaveholders in seeking out their escaping enslaved property. Maryland had a series of its own similar state-level laws. In 1838, the Maryland General Assembly established an act to provide for the recapture of fugitive slaves which formulated that

> *any negro slave who shall escape from this state into the District of Columbia, or into any of the states of this Union against the will and consent of his master or owner, with a view to escape from such servitude, shall upon sufficient evidence of such facts be deemed guilty of felony.*

The act also stipulated that the governor of Maryland became responsible for demanding the return of a freedom seeker from the authorities in the District of Columbia or the governor of the state to which they had fled.

In 1850, a second Federal Fugitive Slave Act was established to strengthen the 1793 act. The updated and strengthened act was a part of the Compromise of 1850. Like its predecessor, it allowed for enslaved people to be seized and returned to their owners when they crossed into another state, but it imposed greater penalties on accomplices. Furthermore, it required that the federal government intervene and restrict enslaved individuals from testifying on their own behalf or having the right to a trial by jury. Both Fugitive Slave Acts greatly impacted free Black communities because they were often targeted by slave catchers looking for reward money associated with capturing escaped slaves.

The Fugitive Slave Act unleashed the slave catchers. *Library of Congress.*

Despite having federal acts to protect the interests of its citizen slaveholders, in 1860, the Maryland Code added additional restrictions such that

> *any person may arrest any runaway negro, and carry him before a judge or justice, and have him committed to the jail of the county; Any judge or justice before whom any negro shall be brought as a runaway, shall commit him to the jail of the county, unless he be satisfied by competent testimony that said negro is free; The sheriff shall, within fifteen days after a negro is committed as a runaway, advertise the same in some daily newspaper published in the city of Baltimore.*

Escaping from Maryland was challenging. Freedom seekers would need to rely heavily on the assistance of enclaves of free Blacks and antislavery religious groups. There were sizable free Black communities in Baltimore City, the counties on the Eastern Shore and in nearby Washington, D.C., as a result of manumissions through self-purchase or by owners after service of a term of years.

Baltimore City, boasting the largest free Black community in the entire country, was an attractive place for freedom seekers to blend in easily without being detected. Freedom seekers fleeing from Montgomery and Prince George's Counties were able to hide at the homes of family members who were a part of the free Black community in nearby Washington, D.C. Since Washington, D.C., was by the Potomac River, its location was advantageous to enslaved individuals hired out to labor there, like sisters Mary and Emily Edmonson of Montgomery County, who would later be part of an attempted escape on the *Pearl* on April 15, 1848.

Black churches were involved in facilitating escapes. The African Methodist Episcopal Church, which was founded by formerly enslaved individuals, was led by ministers along the Eastern Seaboard who had connections to both freedom seekers and the free Black community. Moses Viney noted in interviews that Bishop Alexander Walker Wayman, a close friend of Frederick Douglass and his wife, Anna Murray, had assisted him in escaping once he reached Philadelphia in about 1840.

Freedom seekers also sought and received support from members of the Society of Friends (otherwise known as Quakers) who were known for their antislavery stance and assistance in slave flight. The Quakers outlawed slavery in 1777, and most Quakers adhered to this decision. There were

MARYLAND 1840: COMPARISON OF FREE AND ENSLAVED AFRICAN AMERICANS
TO TOTAL POPULATION BY COUNTY

County	Total Free Blacks and Percentage of Total Population		Total Enslaved Blacks and Percentage of Total Population		Total Population
Allegany	215	1.4%	812	5.2%	15,690
Anne Arundel	5,083	17.2%	9,819	33.2%	29,532
Baltimore	3,486	10.9%	3,199	10.0%	32,066
Baltimore City	17,967	17.5%	4,396	4.3%	102,213
Calvert	1,474	16.0%	4,170	45.2%	9,229
Caroline	1,720	22.0%	752	9.6%	7,806
Carroll	898	5.2%	1,122	6.5%	17,241
Cecil	2,551	14.8%	1,352	7.8%	17,232
Charles	819	5.1%	9,182	57.3%	16,023
Dorchester	3,987	21.2%	4,227	22.4%	18,843
Frederick	2,985	8.2%	4,445	12.2%	36,405
Harford	2,436	14.2%	2,643	15.4%	17,120
Kent	2,491	23.0%	2,735	25.2%	10,842
Montgomery	1,313	9.0%	5,135	35.0%	14,669
Prince George's	1,080	5.5%	10,636	54.4%	19,539
Queen Anne's	2,541	20.1%	3,960	31.3%	12,633
Saint Mary's	1,393	10.5%	5,761	43.6%	13,224
Somerset	2,646	13.5%	5,377	27.6%	19,508
Talbot	2,340	19.4%	3,687	30.5%	12,090
Washington	1,580	5.5%	2,546	8.8%	28,850
Worcester	3,073	16.7%	3,539	19.3%	18,377
Total	62,078	13.2%	89,495	19.1%	469,232

Source: Legacy of Slavery in Maryland. http://slavery.msa.maryland.gov.

PRINCE GEORGE'S COUNTY, SCT : THE STATE OF MARYLAND

To the Sheriff of Prince George's County, Greeting:

You are hereby commanded to take Thomas E Dant

if he *shall be found in your bailiwick, and* him *safe keep, so that you have* his *body before the next Circuit Court for said County, to be held at the Town of Upper Marlborough, in the said County,* on the first Monday in *Immediately* next, *to answer unto the State of Maryland on presentment* and indictment *for* harbouring a runaway negros —

Hereof fail not at your peril, and have you then and there this writ.

Witness the Honorable Peter W. Crain, Judge of the First Judicial Circuit of Maryland, the

day of 185

Issued the 12 *day of* Nov 185 9

Chs Middleton —— *Clerk.*

You are hereby commanded to summon Rich'd Hopkins

to testify for the State of Maryland against Thomas E Dant

Returnable first Monday in ——— 185 Immediately

Chs Middleton , *Clerk.*

To the Sheriff of Prince George's County.

This is an example of a bench warrant for Thomas E. Dant for harboring "runaway negroes." *Collection of Maryland State Archives.*

prominent antislavery Quaker communities in Maryland in the town of Brookeville, in Baltimore City and on the Eastern Shore. Sandy Spring in Montgomery County is often credited as a safe haven for freedom seekers journeying north. Not all Quaker accomplices avoided the notice of their neighbors, however. On Maryland's Eastern Shore in 1857, Arthur Leverton in Caroline County was implicated in assisting Margaret Haskins on her journey to freedom. In 1860, Maryland's House of Delegates scrutinized and called for the arrest of abolitionist Thomas Garrett, in Delaware, after receiving word that his assistance to more than two thousand individuals included some from Maryland.

The Underground Railroad was greatly compromised by the watchful eye of slaveholders and other individuals who exposed its inner workings.

In various Maryland counties, sheriffs patrolled their communities in search of freedom seekers, who were then arrested and jailed, awaiting the return to their owners. Members of the free Black community were faced with false accusations of being escaped slaves. When there was a rise in the number of escapes in the nineteenth century, slave-catching networks grew in number and became just as organized and informed as the state's network of operatives assisting flight. Notorious slave catchers included Thomas McCreary and Patty Cannon.

These slave catchers increasingly became aware of and extended their searches to places such as Baltimore, Pittsburgh, Philadelphia and New York. As an instance of their wide-ranging nets, when Henrietta "Henny" Trusty, mother of Henry Highland Garnet, escaped with a group after her owner William Spencer died, she was caught in New York and jailed. Fortunately, her freedom was negotiated by an agent, and she was manumitted by William Spencer's brother Isaac. Trusty and her family remained in New York until their deaths, while her son Henry Highland Garnet became a recognized figure of the international antislavery movement.

Top: Henrietta Trusty was the mother of Reverend Henry Highland Garnet (pictured here), an abolitionist, editor, temperance leader and diplomat. *National Portrait Gallery, Smithsonian Institution.*

Bottom: James Collins Johnson was betrayed and tried in 1843 as a "fugitive slave." *Princeton University Archives, Department of Rare Books and Special Collections, Princeton University Library.*

Maryland's escaped slaves established communities in the northern United States and Canada. While a large contingent settled in Pennsylvania, Massachusetts and New York, there were also significant numbers in New Jersey. For example,

James Collins Johnson, who fled from his owner near Easton, Maryland, found refuge at Princeton University. New Jersey towns like Camden, Cape May and Salem saw an influx of freedom seekers, who formed communities of people from nearby Maryland locales. While in Cape May before one of her many journeys back to Maryland, Harriet Tubman worked as a cook in hotels, a wage-earning privilege afforded her as a self-liberated woman.

Whether still enslaved, escaping or resettled in the North, African Americans lived in constant fear of being caught and sold south by slave traders. Owners of enslaved people or their estates could sell off "surplus" or offending human chattel in order to make a profit, pay off debts or set an example for others. Sales separated families, even husbands and wives or mothers and babies. In some instances, in Maryland, county sheriffs assisted in the sale of enslaved people who were arrested as runaways. If an owner didn't come to claim the individual as property and the arrested person couldn't prove they were free, the sheriffs had the authority to sell them. Slave traders such as the notorious Hope Slatter, Austin Woolfolk, James Donovan and John Denning were located in Baltimore, ready to ship purchased bondsmen south. Slave catchers supplied those they captured to traders' agents working all over the state. Slave trading and catching became, in many ways, an incendiary operation as enslaved property was sometimes unexpectedly kidnapped. This led to slave catching as a profession being frowned on by Marylanders whose property had been secreted away and sold south.

The struggle for freedom in Maryland was a long, hard fight for the state's enslaved population, who wouldn't have achieved it without the demand for liberty through resistance, the vocality of antislavery supporters and the efforts of those offering refuge that spanned its borders and beyond. Flight from Maryland improved from one generation to the next as the changing economy and

Cash for Negroes.

The highest cash prices, at all times will be given for negroes of both sexes that are slaves for life and good titles. My office is in Pratt Street, between Sharp and Howard streets, and opposite to the Repository where I or my agent can be seen at all times. All persons having negroes to sell would do well to see me before they dispose of them as I am always buying and forwarding to the New Orleans market.— I will also receive and keep negroes at 25 cts. each, per day, and forward them to any Southern market, at the request of the owner. My establishment is large, comfortable and airy, and all above ground, and kept in complete order, with a large yard for exercise and is the strongest and most splendid building of the kind in the United States.— And as the character of my House and Yard is so completely established for strength, comfort and cleanliness, and it being a place where I keep all my own, that I will not be accountable for the future, from any escapes of any kind from my establishment.

HOPE H. SLATTER,
Baltimore.

Feb. 29 1839   1y

Hope Slatter frequently advertised in Maryland newspapers, sometimes describing his slave-trading establishment. *Collection of Maryland State Archives.*

modernizing transportation in cities and towns expanded the pathway to freedom. The inner workings of Maryland's network of individuals who actively participated in the Underground Railroad may never be fully recognized, but there are certainly more names and stories to discover than we currently know. The stories of well-known figures have been around for over one hundred years and are embedded in historical texts and oral histories. However, there are still numerous unsung heroes of flight in Maryland who are unknown or may not be easily discovered due to a lack of documentation associated with the need for anonymity during the time. This book highlight sseveral stories of lesser-known figures and showcases how these narratives can be rescued through research.

Maya D. Davis
Washington, D.C.
March 2022

Chapter 1

SETTING A LEGAL PRECEDENT

ALEXANDER HELMSLEY (QUEEN ANNE'S), MID-1820S

Until the 1820s, Reverend Alexander Helmsley, then known as Nathan Mead, was enslaved in Queen Anne's County, bordering the state of Delaware. Isaac Baggs owned Nathan Mead, and far from presiding over a stereotypically large southern plantation, Baggs owned a 259-acre home farm in Tullies Neck, called Hawkins Pharsalia, and about 365 additional acres. He held fewer than fifteen bondsmen between 1800 and 1820 and mentioned only eight enslaved African Americans in his 1833 will.

Late in life, when interviewed, Reverend Alexander Helmsley remembered that the main characteristic distinguishing Baggs was his hypocrisy. His weekday treatment of those he enslaved was not consistent with his Sunday preaching. When catechizing African Americans, to benefit himself, Baggs emphasized honesty and obedience if the African Americans wished to enjoy life on earth and in heaven.

What Reverend Helmsley remembered about himself was his wish for liberty in order to have freedom of thought and to realize his ideas. He delayed escaping due to his friends' and family's fears of ruin. When twenty-three, Nathan Mead finally ran away, taking advantage of his usual weekend visit to friends seven miles off the farm. His friends were unsuspecting, because he often threatened to leave without acting on the threat.

Mead's goal was New Jersey, a place easily reached by land or by water. Its attractions were common knowledge among freedom seekers on the Eastern Shore. In his autobiography, Samuel Ringgold Ward, a prominent Marylander who grew up in New Jersey and New York, wrote of his family's escape from the Eastern Shore in 1820:

> At the time…it was not always necessary to go to Canada; they [his parents] therefore did as the few who then left mostly did—aim for a Free State, and settle among Quakers.….Accordingly, obtaining the best directions they could, they set out for Cumberland County, in the State of New Jersey, where they had learned slavery did not exist—Quakers lived in numbers, who would afford the escaped any and every protection consistent with their peculiar tenets—and where a number of blacks lived, who in cases of emergency could and would make common cause with and for each other.

Mead echoed Ward, saying New Jersey was "where I had been told, people were free, and nobody would disturb me." Like the Ward family, he looked to the Quakers who were scattered across Maryland, Delaware, New Jersey and Pennsylvania and were easily identified by their dress and speech. After travelling thirty-three miles, Mead encountered someone he called "a good old Quaker," with whom he stayed for three weeks. From the Quaker's home, Mead passed through Philadelphia but did not stay long. He eagerly crossed the Delaware River to New Jersey, reaching Cooper's Creek safely. He spent two months there.

New Jersey, however, still practiced slavery, although in a form different than Maryland's. In 1804, New Jersey's new gradual emancipation law only gave freedom to those born after 1804 when they reached a given age. It permitted term and lifelong slavery to coexist, resulting in New Jersey's form of slavery lasting well beyond slavery in nearby northern states.

Mead settled in West Jersey, which differed from East Jersey in the form of agriculture, extent of slavery and attitudes of many Whites. In West Jersey, Quakers had eliminated most slavery and had advanced African American freedom using the tactic of lawsuits.

New Jersey revised its slave code in 1821, around the time Mead arrived. Slave catchers were increasingly invading New Jersey. Their invasions had raised the question of balancing the personal liberties of all residents against the fulfillment of the constitutional duty to return those called "fugitive slaves." New Jersey now imposed a hefty fine and a sentence of hard labor on someone "wrongfully" returning a person to a slave state.

In 1826, New Jersey passed the first personal liberty law, pitting states' rights against federal law. In contrast to the 1793 Fugitive Slave Act, the personal liberty law required a warrant for arrest and a hearing, before a judge could issue the "certificate of removal" needed to return a "fugitive slave" to a slave state.

Unaware of these developments, Mead moved from Cooper's Creek north to Evesham in Burlington County. He perhaps lived in one of the communities of color where freedom seekers tended to concentrate. Following his uncle's example, under the tutelage of church elders, he went through conversion to the African Methodist Episcopal Church in 1823 and in 1827 was licensed to preach.

Mead married a woman named Nancy in 1821, and they had three children. Nancy had come to Evesham because in Maryland she had a tenuous freedom, legitimated by word of mouth rather than formal papers. Her parents had been enslaved in Delaware but were freed verbally before her birth. Nancy and her mother had migrated to Caroline County, Maryland, following Richard Cooper, son of their former owner. With her mother's consent, Nancy had spent her childhood with Cooper. When a teenager, she ran away in the summer of 1824. Later New Jersey court papers would describe her with "a small scar on one of her cheeks…tolerably well built, rather dark complected…upwards of five feet high." The court papers also stated, "It was supposed that she was pregnant when she ran away," making Cooper's treatment of her suspect.

Nancy and Nathan lived peacefully for about nine years in an area with other Maryland freedom seekers. Tempted by what Nathan called "favorable offers [of work]," the family made the mistake of moving from Evesham to Northampton (near Mount Holly). There, they were located by a slave speculator in October 1835.

Before moving to Northampton, Nathan had heard news that someone from his former owner's family was pursuing him. He did not know, though, that Isaac Baggs had died nor that a man named John Willoughby was acting as agent for executor Goldsborough Price. Not coincidentally, Willoughby also represented Richard D. Cooper from Delaware's Kent County, the man who laid claim to Nancy and her freeborn children.

If he located Mead, the slave hunter had to communicate with a local official about his allegations before the official could order an arrest. Goldsborough Price swore in writing that "Nathan a Negro man" was the property of Isaac Baggs. The Burlington County Lower Court judge, George Haywood, issued the warrant, and a Northampton constable,

Charles Bryan, executed it. Bryan took Mead to court in the Burlington County seat, Mount Holly, on October 24, 1835. Unfortunately for Mead, Haywood was a proslavery Virginian by birth.

Mead's capture was unexpected. A group of White southerners had been hanging around his house for several days, pretending to hunt. Having bought title to Mead "running," they were actually reconnoitering in hopes of a capture. One morning, Mead got up and opened the door, preparing to go to work. He later remembered that the local constable went into Mead's house, grabbed him and exclaimed, "You are my prisoner!" The constable then explained that he had a warrant to bring Mead, alias "Alexander Helmsley," to court. The southerners followed the constable into the house and handcuffed Mead, or rather Helmsley, as he was now known locally.

During these events, Helmsley prudently did not admit that he had escaped. Fearful that the constable and the southerners would kidnap him to Maryland, Helmsley sent for his employer. The employer came to Mead's house and prevailed on the constable to pledge to take Helmsley to court. Off Helmsley went in a carriage, escorted by two armed southerners. One southerner was a witness named Booker who harassed Helmsley in order to make him admit their acquaintance. At the courthouse, Judge Haywood informed Helmsley that he was alleged to have escaped from Isaac Baggs and threatened Helmsley with a return to slavery if the allegation were substantiated. The sheriff put Helmsley in jail until an initial hearing in court before the judge.

The slave catchers also captured Nancy and the children. Luckily, antislavery activists found the Helmsleys a Pennsylvania Abolition Society defense team. It was headed by David Paul Brown, whom a Vermont newspaper described as "the eminent abolitionist lawyer of Philadelphia." Both sides stretched the trial out to give themselves time to prepare their cases. The Helmsleys' defense obtained a postponement until November 24, 1835, and the other side countered with another delay until December 9. The sheriff, meanwhile, kept Alexander Helmsley languishing in jail in Mount Holly for lack of bail.

Well-known lawyer David Paul Brown spent many years defending African Americans in the Philadelphia area. *Library Company of Philadelphia.*

December 9 and the days following were tense. The witnesses and evidence presented by each side were contradictory. Booker and his brother testified to Alexander Helmsley's identity, allegedly having known him when he was young and enslaved. They could not, however, specify any distinguishing marks. On October 23, 1835, the lawyer presented the claimant's certificate for return to the owner, which described Nathan Mead as "a light complected negro of middling stature about 30 years of age—thick lips, broad nose, and no particular scar or mark observed on his face." In court on October 28, in contrast, an affidavit was presented describing him when he escaped as "of a dark complexion."

The Booker brothers stretched their credibility when they swore to Nancy's enslaved status. She had belonged to a different owner than Alexander's and had not known Alexander before they met in New Jersey. The claimant's side lacked a bill of sale and thus was unable to establish title of ownership of Alexander. The Meads' lawyer countered by presenting Isaac Baggs's will, which had a clause desiring that all his African Americans be freed at a certain age. They also provided a Baggs estate inventory omitting "Nathan Mead."

On December 10 and 11, a number of Evesham residents contradicted the Booker testimony. White Quakers Josiah Roberts and David Davis affirmed the Helmsleys' residence in New Jersey at the time the Helmsleys were alleged to be enslaved, and so also swore several Blacks, Charles, Perry and Elizabeth Gibson and Ariadne Johnson.

It was agreed that the judge would sum up the cases of Nancy and Alexander Helmsley together on December 23. That left the Helmsleys and their defense to worry until right before Christmas. The Helmsley defense was not idle during the intervening two weeks. They expeditiously procured needed documents through the fervor of Thomas Shipley (Shipleigh), a Quaker lawyer and enthusiastic advocate for African Americans.

Shipley secretly traveled to obtain evidence of the manumission of Nancy's mother, authenticated by the governor or chief justice of Delaware in Dover. The defense wanted to prove, first, that John Cooper, Nancy's mother's former owner, had never transferred ownership of Nancy's mother to anyone else and, second, that Nancy's mother was freed before Nancy's birth. If Nancy's mother were not enslaved, neither were any children born subsequently. Successful, Shipley disregarded exhaustion from the rushed trip in order to return as quickly as he could.

Before collapsing with illness, Shipley delivered the papers to the sheriff, just when the defense could delay no longer. For added weight, the defense had been arguing that since Nancy had moved from Delaware to Maryland with her owner's permission, such an interstate transfer meant that Nancy was free under Maryland law. It was presentation of the proofs of manumission that forced the grudging concession from Judge Haywood that Nancy and therefore her children were not enslaved.

The wily defense, however, had had to scheme not only to free Nancy and the children but also to provide for the contingency that Alexander himself might not be freed. To rescue him from return to Maryland, they sent Shipley on another exhausting trip, this time to Newark for special writs from New Jersey's chief justice. The habeas corpus writ would counter the certificate issued by Judge Haywood allowing Goldsborough's agent to take Alexander to Maryland. Instead, it required Alexander to appear in the state supreme court. The other writ or *certiorari* would call for the supreme court's reexamination of the lower court's decision, providing hope that the supreme court would override it.

The indefatigable Shipley traveled all night and reached the chief justice's residence before he was out of bed the next morning. Even so, Shipley's urgency convinced the chief justice to issue the necessary writs and order their delivery to the sheriff in Mount Holly. The sheriff arrived in court just as the crowd of spectators, sympathetic to the Helmsleys, was awaiting Judge Haywood's decision. To the crowd's delight, the writs surprised and embarrassed Judge Haywood just as he was pronouncing Nancy's discharge and Alexander's return to slavery. The writs took the final decision on Alexander's liberty out of Haywood's hands and placed it in those of New Jersey Supreme Court chief justice Joseph C. Hornblower.

Thankfully, Nancy and the children were at liberty, but the sheriff again took custody of Alexander until the next supreme court term. While Alexander spent three months suffering in Mount Holly's jail, the nightmare of a return to slavery haunted him. Aside from the supreme court's decision, there was still a strong possibility that the claimant would try to divert the party into Maryland, where Judge Haywood's certificate could take effect. When the authorities finally conveyed Alexander

Chief Justice Joseph Hornblower was not yet known as an abolitionist in 1836. *Semi-Centennial Celebration of the New Jersey Historical Society at Newark, N.J., May 16, 1895.*

to Trenton, the defense team sent two lawyers against the claimant's one and made sure their lawyers carried pistols. The group, however, arrived in Trenton without incident.

Because of Thomas Shipley's further intervention, Theodore Frelinghuysen now led the defense before the supreme court. Frelinghuysen was a gifted lawyer with political clout from previous service as a state attorney general and a United States senator. He presented a brilliant argument on Alexander's behalf. On March 3, 1836, the justices decided *State v. Sheriff of Burlington County* in Alexander's favor, and he was released.

Chief Justice Hornblower's 1836 decision set an important, if unnoticed, precedent. It not only reaffirmed a decision in *Stoutenborough v. Haviland* earlier in 1836, which stated color did not necessarily equate with enslavement in New Jersey. It also implied that the Fugitive Slave Act of 1793 was unconstitutional.

Hornblower, however, was careful not to bring up the federal law, preferring to focus on New Jersey's 1826 Personal Liberty Law. Hornblower declared that the 1826 state law left open the possibility of a resident being taken out of state under the pretext of slavery. As a result, he ruled all residents were presumed to be freeborn or, in accordance with the state constitution, should have their freedom determined by a jury trial allowing possible appeal.

Chief Justice Hornblower's ruling was surprising. He was not yet known as an abolitionist or even as antislavery. He had owned African Americans before the 1820s. Like Frelinghuysen, he had promoted removal of freedmen abroad through colonization.

The radical ruling, however, reflected the current situation in New Jersey. By the 1830s, free African Americans had reached the tipping point in terms of numbers, economic resources and creation of their own institutions. They were now starting to stand up for their rights. The crowd present for Judge Haywood's dire ruling would have included free Blacks among those described by abolitionist William Still as "friends of humanity…assembled from all parts. Many…personally acquainted with the prisoner."

The Hornblower decision was a relief but did not guarantee Alexander Helmsley's freedom, given the trial's local notoriety. Helmsley reluctantly took his friends' advice to avoid another attempt at kidnapping. He braved storms and cold while walking most of the two hundred miles to Otsego County, New York. Because of the hard journey, he fell sick when he arrived. Once he recovered, his family joined him, and when the weather permitted, they continued to Farmington on Lake Ontario. There, Helmsley heeded foreboding dreams, like those he had when he was escaping from Maryland. The Helmsleys took the precaution of traveling to Toronto by way of Rochester, not Farmington. From Rochester, they crossed Lake Ontario on a British boat, *The Traveller*. Once in Canada, Helmsley finally felt that "my shackles were struck off, and that a man was a man by law."

Canada offered freedom but was not necessarily a welcoming place or one in which to thrive. The Helmsley family lost the comforts they were used to in New Jersey. They had to start anew, in Reverend Helmsley's terms, "among strangers, poverty-stricken, and in a cold country." Without help in Toronto and accustomed to farm work, Alexander Helmsley chose rural St. Catharines. In comparison with New Jersey, winters were long, rents high and agricultural prices low. Helmsley could not make a living from the land he farmed and had to resort to day labor.

For years, Alexander Helmsley nursed the hope of returning to New Jersey, which he considered home, but newspapers constantly confirmed the risk. So, he committed himself to Canada and the growing town of St. Catharines, situated by the newly built Welland Canals connecting Lakes

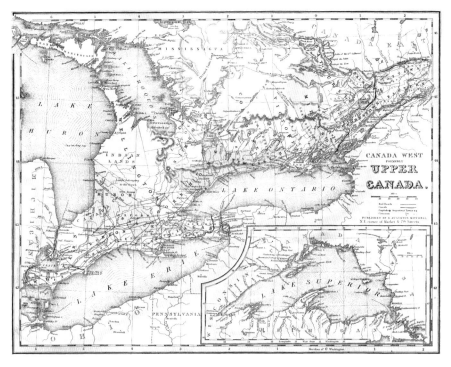

Many African Americans fled from the United States to Upper Canada. *St. Catharines Museum—1979.3.11.*

Erie and Ontario. He participated as a volunteer in the Coloured Corps for twelve days in 1837 during the unsuccessful but historic MacKenzie Rebellion, which opposed British rule in Upper Canada. In 1848, Helmsley took his oath as a British citizen, Canada still being British territory.

Two of the Helmsley children died in Canada, and Alexander Helmsley faced illness and accumulated debts. Helmsley, however, found solace in his faith and committed himself to the Lord's work. He became associated with the African Methodist Episcopal Church and served in St. Catharines at the second AME Church, Bethel Chapel. He participated in the 1840 African Methodist Episcopal Canadian conference that was held in Toronto, at which he was ordained a deacon.

Reverend Helmsley made a point of ministering to other American refugees, of whom there was a growing number. By 1855, out of a total population of six thousand inhabitants in St. Catharines, about eight hundred were African Americans, of whom almost all adults were formerly enslaved. In St. Catharines, a close-knit community of Eastern Shore refugees grew up, including Harriet Tubman and her family, who came in the 1850s.

Reverend Alexander Helmsley's contribution to the African Methodist Episcopal churches in Canada was recognized when he was ordained as an elder and given a salary. He continued traveling as a circuit rider until February 1854, when he became afflicted with dropsy. He proudly remembered:

> *I have served the people in the provinces as a minister in the Methodist persuasion for some twenty years. My pay has been little.…My mind has ever been to trust the Lord. I have never prayed for wealth nor honor, but only to guide his church and do his will.*

Reverend Helmsley died on November 15, 1855, while in his sixties. In Upper Canada, he is revered as a "Black Pioneer."

Reverend Helmsley's story was not preserved outside the family because of the Hornblower decision, which received little recognition until the passage of the 1850 Fugitive Slave Act. However, there are several primary sources. A Quaker weekly, *The Friend*, published an article in 1836 giving a detailed report on the trial. The author, "S.," could have been Thomas Shipley, whose assiduous efforts on behalf of the Helmsleys were recorded by William Still in *The Underground Railroad* in 1872.

But it was Benjamin Drew who captured the most information on Reverend Helmsley's life when taking down the words of freedom seekers for *A North-*

Side View of Slavery, published in 1856. Drew interviewed Reverend Helmsley during his travels through Canada investigating the lives of transplanted freedom seekers. Reverend Helmsley told Drew how he judged the freedom he had found in Canada:

> *We were then making both ends meet. I then made up my mind that salt and potatoes in Canada were better than pound-cake and chickens in a state of suspense and anxiety in the United States. Now I am a regular Britisher.*

Chapter 2

CURIOUS PLACES OF REFUGE

Moses Viney (Talbot), 1840

On August 8, 1840, Richard K. Murphy of Easton, Talbot County, Maryland, advertised in the *Easton Gazette* for his enslaved African American Perry Thomas. The advertisement described Perry, who had fled "Sunday last," as:

> *24 or 25 years of age, about five feet high, not very black, with a scar on his upper lip; had on when he ranaway* [sic] *blue trowsers and jacket, and had with him a white roundabout* [short, close-fitting jacket] *and white pantaloon, a new pair of shoes and black fur hat.*

The advertisement offered a $50 reward if he were taken in-state and $150 otherwise.

This freedom seeker would become known as "Moses Viney" in Schenectady, New York. Upon Moses Viney's death, an obituary called him "one of Schenectady's most interesting and picturesque characters." Until Moses Viney died, generations of alumni of Union College in Schenectady considered him to be "part of the[ir] famous institution." They knew Moses Viney as a genial and constant companion to Eliphalet Nott, who was president of Union College for a record-breaking sixty-two years. After Nott's death, Moses Viney continued his association with Union College until his own death in 1909.

$150 Reward.

Runaway from the subscriber on Sunday last, a negro man named

PERRY THOMAS

24 or 25 years of age, about five feet high, not very black, with a scar on his upper lip; had on when he ranaway blue trowsers and jacket, and had with him a white roundabout and white pantaloons, a new pair of shoes and black fur hat.

I will give 50 dollars reward if taken in the State, and $150 if taken out of the State and secured in Easton jail so that I get him again.

RICHARD K. MURPHY.
Easton, June 13th, 1840.

This runaway advertisement documents Schenectady articles on Moses Viney. *Collection of the Maryland State Archives.*

During his years on campus, Moses Viney knew hundreds of students. He gratified them through his talent at recalling names and faces. At college events where he was present, alumni came over, eager to shake his hand and reminisce. Viney could relate to them at length college tales of pranks and of those who became famous, like President Chester Arthur. The college community respected Viney. A North Carolina reporter wrote in 1905 that five hundred White "judges, clergymen, men distinguished in all walks of life, rose to their feet and cheered" Viney at a Union College alumni gathering.

The details of Moses Viney's life are dramatic, but by the time Viney became an elderly celebrity of sorts, he or those relating his past were taking liberties with details. Viney's story of escape and attainment of freedom appeared in Union College publications, starting in 1895 when Viney was seventy-eight. By 1895, Nott had been dead about thirty years, and Viney had been in Schenectady for fifty-five years. Viney was flattered by interviews, the repeated publication of his picture and the number of his prominent acquaintances. Reporters used interviews with Viney to write articles on occasions like Viney's ninety-first birthday.

Regardless of how beloved at Union College Viney became, he was always in the difficult position of an African American man on a White campus. Viney maintained a positive image through his smile, dignity and dress. The 1910 *Garnet* called him one of "the now nearly extinct type of old school negro, who as slaves had received their training during antebellum days." Viney escaped Maryland to leave behind his enslaved condition, yet after the Civil War, he must have felt White Schenectady expected him to continue an association with slavery. During the nostalgic end of the nineteenth century, it was precisely Viney's rescue from slavery that made a northerner like Nott into a hero.

As told in Schenectady, Moses Viney ended up in the city by chance. On March 10, 1817, he was born in Trappe, which was in Talbot County on the Chesapeake Bay's Eastern Shore. Called "Perry Thomas," he was the eldest of Horace Thomas's twenty-one children. Perry (as he will be called here until he changed his name) knew his birthday because he was a playmate of Richard K. Murphy, who was exactly one year older.

Moses Viney built a thriving business as a carriage driver. *Courtesy of Special Collections, Picture File, Schaffer Library, Union College.*

In the background, a view of nondenominational Union College, founded in 1795. *Courtesy of Special Collections, Picture File, Schaffer Library, Union College.*

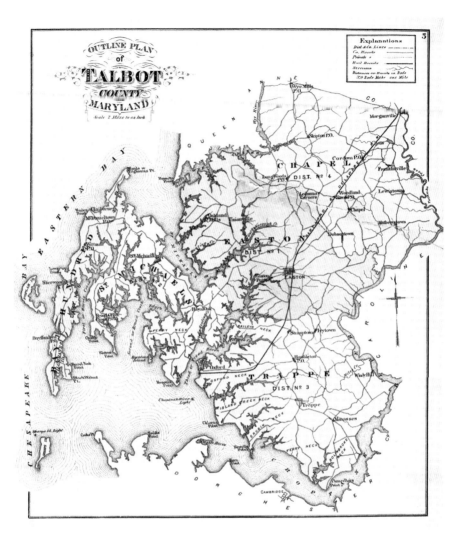

This 1877 map shows Trappe, Talbot County, the home of Moses Viney's first owner, William Murphy. *Talbot Historical Society.*

William Murphy was the father of Richard and the owner of Perry. Perry remained Richard's companion until he was sent to the fields at age seven. Perry was fourteen in 1831, when William died. At the time of settling William's estate, the distribution of property separated Perry from his parents.

Perry's former playmate Richard K. Murphy became his new owner. Richard's childhood with Perry did not stand in the way of Richard's calculating Perry's cash value. While working as a butler for Richard, Perry overheard a conversation about Richard's possible plans to sell him. Perry decided to flee. As a Union College alumnus put it, Perry was motivated because "within the slave there was a native instinct of liberty, a craving for a man's dignity, a dissatisfaction with things unworthy." The college's 1910 *Garnet* stated, "With an ambitious temperament and more than ordinary native intelligence, he naturally longed for freedom."

Perry had prepared for escape. He had a destination learned from the saying, "The wild geese come from Canada where all are free." He had a twenty-dollar "liberty fund" saved from winning pennies for stacking wheat sheaves at harvest. Perry knew local geography because his owner had sent him around on errands.

In contradiction to the runaway advertisement, college accounts said Perry prudently picked Easter (April 19, 1840) to escape. As was customary, he had a day's holiday and could obtain permission to leave the estate to celebrate a festival on Sunday and Monday. Escaping on Easter gave Perry lead time before people at Perry's homeplace would raise the alarm about his disappearance. To avoid capture, Perry had taken the precaution of befriending the Murphy bloodhounds. When his pursuers set the bloodhounds on Perry, Perry remained unharmed and sent the dogs home.

Perry mentioned two companions in flight but never identified them. Judging by their places and dates of escape, Hinson Piney and Washington Brooks may well have been Perry's fellow freedom seekers. They came from nearby Easton and Island Creek Neck and escaped about April 11 and Easter, respectively.

Before they left, Perry and his companions swore they would choose death over capture. On the first day, Perry and his two companions traveled seventeen miles northeast to Denton in Caroline County. After passing through the town by night, they rested and continued on. Because patrollers monitored the bridge across the Choptank River, by night, the freedom seekers improvised. They used fence rails to row a "borrowed" canoe across the river, just as had been done by William Green, another 1840 freedom seeker from Oxford Neck.

Delaware, yet another slave state, lay between the freedom seekers and freedom in Philadelphia. Perhaps, as in the case of Green, the trio traveled with Underground Railroad help. They went by stage to Smyrna, Delaware, where the Delaware River meets the Delaware Bay. Daringly, Perry and his friends managed to board the steamboat up the Delaware River to Philadelphia without presenting freedom papers or an owner's written permission.

In Philadelphia, the freedom seekers stopped long enough to get shelter and advice from Reverend Alexander Walker Wayman at Mother Bethel African Episcopal Methodist Church. The future bishop was from Caroline County, neighboring Perry's home county on Maryland's Eastern Shore.

Armed with a letter from abolitionists in Philadelphia, the group proceeded to another major Underground Railroad stop, New York City. From there, they again traveled by water, heading up the Hudson River. Directed by New York sympathizers, their destinations were Troy and then Canada. However, in Troy, they were unable to find the owner of the canalboat line that would take them to Canada. As a Union College account put it, they "wandered" on to Schenectady.

BISHOP ALEXANDER W. WAYMAN, D. D.

Alexander Walker Wayman from Caroline County became a well-known bishop of the African Methodist Episcopal Church. *Florida State Archives.*

Now in the North, Perry took a freedom name, Moses Viney. He presumably chose Moses in deference to the biblical leader who brought the Israelites out of slavery in Egypt. In order to make a living, Moses Viney turned to the agricultural and domestic skills he had learned while enslaved. Viney was amazed to receive five dollars a month in Glenville (Scotia) doing farmwork for Dr. Alexander Glen Fonda for about seven years. Fonda also found Viney's two companions jobs as laborer and gardener.

Viney switched jobs to work as servant for nine months for John and James Corcoran. In 1847, probably because Dr. Fonda was an alumnus of Union College, the president of the college, Eliphalet Nott, hired Viney. Viney became a combination of domestic servant, messenger and driver of the president's famed three-wheeled "chariot."

Moses Viney found a protector and role model in President Nott, and President Nott found a hardworking, loyal companion and confidant in Viney. In addition to the employer-employee relationship, they built a friendship based on trust and respect. They became mutually dependent by the end of Nott's life.

The relationship, however, was unequal, given the difference in status, education and wealth. After all, Viney was a friendless refugee from slavery. To Nott's contemporaries, Nott was admirable for treating Viney as a Christian equal. One of Nott's admirers, Tayler Lewis, wrote of the relationship, "No better proof could be given of the perfect and undeniable manhood of the one [Viney], the essential goodness and greatness of the other [Nott]."

After the 1850 Fugitive Slave Act, Moses Viney lived in fear of slave catchers. There was a double risk. Either Union College's southern students or one of Nott's enemies among the "Cotton" Whigs (supporters of the act) might call in the slave catchers. Viney happened to notice his former owner, Richard Murphy, at Given's Hotel in Schenectady. As a result, Viney panicked and confessed his enslaved condition to Nott.

It was prudent for Viney to leave for Canada on the Underground Railroad. Nott gave him more than advice by providing Viney with a document, dated December 5, 1850. It contained a recommendation as well as permission to draw up to one hundred dollars from Nott's bank account. The glowing recommendation for Viney read: "He is a man of great integrity, and great industry and capability. He is a moral and religious man in whom entire confidence can be placed." It was convincing enough for Viney to get two years of work for a member of parliament in Canada.

Nott wanted a resolution to Viney's precarious situation so Viney could return to his job and his wife. Nott and others saw to it that Nott's grandson was sent to Maryland to negotiate Viney's freedom. Viney's owner, Murphy, finally had to capitulate, since Viney was already free in Canada. Nott's grandson convinced him to accept $120, not the $1,600 that Murphy initially requested. In the spring of 1852, Viney returned to Schenectady to pay off what he literally and figuratively owed to Nott. Nott may have advanced the money, but Viney worked hard to pay back the price of his freedom.

For over twenty-five years, Viney devotedly served Nott in a variety of capacities—coachman, messenger, masseur, valet, cook and nurse. Viney made himself indispensable until the president's death in 1866. He spent hours with Nott while Nott was crippled by rheumatism and suffered a series of strokes between 1859 and 1864. Despite the cold and snow, Viney even remained as the very last mourner at Nott's grave after his burial.

For Viney's devotion, the president's will rewarded Viney with the sizeable bequest of $1,000. In the role of an old family retainer, Viney continued to work for the president's widow, Urania Nott, as gardener, coachman and watchman. Urania died in 1886. After Urania's death, Viney cared for the Nott family house, horse and carriage while the Nott litigation with the will dragged on. It was then that Viney began to drive ladies to and from their visits to one another in order to earn enough to feed the horse.

Left: Moses Viney never expected to find refuge on a college campus. *Courtesy of Special Collections, Picture File, Schaffer Library, Union College.*

Right: Eliphalet Nott set a record by being a college president for sixty-two years. *Courtesy of Special Collections, Picture File, Schaffer Library, Union College.*

Viney impressed his customers. They advised him to continue, and so he started what turned out to be a profitable business. Viney inherited the president's unusual three-wheeled carriage from Urania Nott and purchased the Nott horse. He drove alumni, professors and local ladies, as well as visiting luminaries. He charged reasonable rates but, at the same time, took advantage of the absence of streetcars in Schenectady.

As long as he could still work, Viney made driving his livelihood. Due to his broad Schenectady clientele, in 1903, he felt compelled to write a letter to the local *Daily Union* to announce his retirement. He wished to thank the Schenectady citizens for their patronage and, at the same time, to brag a little about his reliability and punctuality. The publication of the letter itself was an achievement for an African American or a domestic servant. It, however, does not necessarily mean Viney could read and write, as the only known handwriting by Viney is a shaky signature on his will.

Just to make sure the public had not forgotten the Nott connection, in his letter, Viney attributed his punctuality to Nott. In fact, Viney became a keeper of Union College memories at the same time as being himself a part of college lore. By the time Viney retired from the livery business at eighty-four, he had decorated his house with what the *Schenectady Gazette* called "sacred keepsakes" of Eliphalet Nott. Viney treasured an etching of Nott, a chair, a cane, a cocked hat and a whiffletree (crossbar) from the Nott carriage.

Although Union College publications and local newspapers focused on Moses Viney and his relationship with the college, there was more to Viney than what he was to the college community. He had an obvious pride in his reputation and enjoyed his friendship with the Nott family, but he also loved his wife and sister. He had a family life and social activities with his wife and, eventually, with his sister and her family.

Viney's political interests are suggested by the listing of his name on a call for a "national colored convention." The convention would be held in Syracuse in October 1864, although he was not listed among the delegates. It became a significant meeting of Black leaders seeking rights. It occurred while African American troops were fighting in the Civil War, during discussion of the Thirteenth Amendment and just before the presidential election.

Viney was shrewd. He converted a job for the college president and a bequest into a taxi service. He then managed his money so he could retire. He bought and resold three plots of land. Even after Nott and his wife died, Viney cultivated the "interest" of Mrs. Raymond, the wife of the next college president. As a result, she included him in the presidential reception for commencement, keeping his college connection alive.

There is no evidence to show how Viney fit into the small local African American community, which in 1865 consisted of 74 Blacks in the city and 110 in the county. He met his wife in Schenectady, but it is unknown where. A fire destroyed the records of the Schenectady Black church he might have attended, so it is not known whether Viney, his wife or his sister were members. Viney was buried from Christ Episcopal Church.

Viney was not marginalized from the White community like others in Schenectady's African American community. In the 1855 New York State Census, he and his wife are listed as "servants" in the Nott household, in contrast to most Blacks with menial jobs, who lived in Ward 3. For decades, Viney and his wife lived on campus, away from the Black community, in a house provided by the college president. It was only when Viney received the bequest from Nott that he purchased the house at 220 Lafayette Street where he lived until he died.

The Schenectady Underground Railroad may have helped Viney, but there is no evidence that he was active in it. Nonetheless, Schenectady's African

American community was active in Black rights and antislavery activities. It had Black and White contacts outside the city. Schenectady barbers Richard P.G. Wright and his son Theodore Sedgwick Wright were members of the New York Vigilance Committee, as well as the only African Americans in Schenectady to belong to St. George's Masonic Lodge. Richard Wright was one of the founders of the city's Antislavery Society in 1838 and attended regional meetings. He helped freedom seeker Charles Nelson escape from Schenectady to Vermont.

Anna (also called Diana) and Leila were key to Viney's family life. Moses Viney had married Anna, a local African American woman, by 1855, but he and Anna had no children. Toward the end of his life, Viney was stricken with rheumatism like his benefactor and restricted to his home. Just as Moses Viney had taken faithful care of Eliphalet Nott during his final illness, Viney's youngest sister, Leila Viney Bond, became Viney's caretaker and heir. He and his wife raised her like a daughter (as she was listed in the census twice).

Leila was one of the last of Moses Viney's Maryland family, although Horace Thomas Viney (a brother or a nephew) also inherited from Viney. Moses Viney brought Leila back to Schenectady from Maryland when she was four years old. After a twenty-five-year absence, Viney returned to his place of enslavement in 1866. Due to the Civil War's toll, there were only a few members of Viney's extensive family left. In addition to his little sister and two or three brothers, he found his father alive. He learned that other brothers had died serving in the United States Colored Troops.

Despite Anna Viney's death in 1885 at age seventy-one, the 1905 New York State Census recorded that Moses Viney had a houseful. Living with him were his sister Leila; Leila's daughter Renefor J. Allen and her husband, Charles J. Allen; Leila's granddaughter Leila M. Allen; and a roomer, Mary F. Cook.

Viney continued to be active after his retirement in 1903. Toward the end of his life, when he could no longer stroll to nearby Crescent Park, he took pleasure in his sister's two grandchildren, in the views from his windows and in communing with his memories. He died in 1909.

Recently, a group in Schenectady and Maryland revived Moses Viney's memory and recognized him as an Underground Railroad hero. In order to emphasize the diversity in local history for his high school students, Neil Yetwin investigated Moses Viney's history and located his grave in a segregated part of Schenectady's Vale Cemetery. Yetwin wrote a series on Viney's life in the *Schenectady County Historical Society Newsletter*.

Reading the series, a *Schenectady Gazette* reporter was inspired to publish an article. That brought Viney to the attention of a coalition that would also become an advocate for promoting Viney's history. The efforts of Dr. Gretchel Hathaway (then Dean of Diversity and Inclusion and Chief Diversity Officer at Union College) led to a 2009 Union College Founders Day celebration of the college's role in abolitionism. Historian James McPherson presented a lecture. In addition, the college unveiled a portrait of Moses Viney painted by Simmie Knox and contributed toward a gravestone where Viney is buried. The gravestone is in the "Ancestral Burial Ground," part of the African American section of Vale Cemetery. Walter Simpkins, involved in the gravestone efforts, began an annual Juneteenth reenactment of Moses Viney at the cemetery.

Dr. Hathaway traveled to Maryland, where she met with the county tourist office and the historical society. That led to a historical marker in Denton where Viney crossed the Choptank River when fleeing. In 2016, Dr. Hathaway published a novel, *A Bonded Friendship: Moses and Eliphalet*, celebrating the unique relationship between President Eliphalet Nott and Moses Viney.

BASIL DORSEY (FREDERICK), 1836

It took a group of geographically separated historians in Maryland (Dean Herrin), Massachusetts (Bambi Miller and Steve Strimer) and Pennsylvania (Chris Densmore) to show that the Ephraim Costly born enslaved in Libertytown, Maryland, was the same man as Basil Dorsey, buried in Florence, Massachusetts. This man's life can be divided into parts—enslavement in Libertytown, Maryland, under the name of Ephraim Costly; travel as a freedom seeker fleeing from Libertytown to Bucks County, Pennsylvania; appearance in court in Doylestown, Pennsylvania; and life as a free man in Florence, Massachusetts. Ephraim became called Basil by the time he was tried in Doylestown, Pennsylvania.

Basil Dorsey's escape from slavery was due to what his eulogist called his attributes of intelligence, "of great physical strength…of iron will, [and] of great force of character." It must have taken all of his pluck and strength of character, along with the energizing effect of liberty, to build a new life twice.

Dorsey's life began about 1810. Since he was called Ephraim Costly in slavery, he will be so called here until he changed his name after his escape.

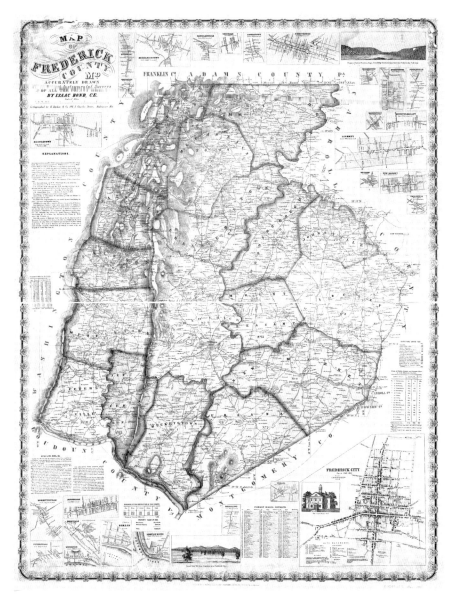

Above: Dorsey's birthplace in Libertytown (Liberty) appears on this 1858 Frederick County map from E. Sachse & Co. *Library of Congress.*

Opposite: The Sabrett Sollers House is an example of nineteenth-century Baltimore County architecture. *Courtesy of the Maryland Historical Trust.*

Ephraim, his parents and his siblings lived on a farm in Libertytown, Frederick County. They were enslaved by Sabrett Sollers, who owned a total of twenty-three enslaved African Americans in 1834. Although Dorsey later referred to an enslaved father, he was of mixed race, a "mulatto." Sabrett may have been the biological parent of the Costly brothers. Or, by one means or another, one of their grandfathers may have been an Englishman married to an African American woman.

Ephraim first appears on an inventory taken when Sabrett died in July 1834. On the list along with Ephraim (age twenty-six) was Louisa (age twenty-two). This woman was probably the same Louisa who became Ephraim's wife and the mother of his first three children. There were six other men between twenty and thirty—like Ephraim, appraised at $300—of whom three must have been the brothers who would flee with him: Solomon (thirty), Daniel (twenty-eight), Alfred (twenty-four), Jerry (twenty-two), Jacob (twenty) and John (eighteen).

As he grew to be a man, Ephraim could not abide slavery. Perhaps because of a promise or his ancestry, he expected his freedom when Sabrett died. Sabrett's son Thomas, however, purchased Ephraim on September 9, 1834. Louisa's owner became Richard Coale, a neighboring slave owner. Ephraim found Coale to be sympathetic and willing to post bond so Ephraim could buy himself. When Thomas Sollers raised the price from $350 to $500, Ephraim could no longer tolerate life with Thomas. Three of Ephraim's brothers decided to join him as he shared in Coale's anger and took Coale's suggestion "to [look to] his legs and try their virtue." It was Saturday night, May 14, 1836.

Ephraim and his brothers overcame any concern for those left behind, although Louisa was about to give birth. On foot, the four Costly brothers bravely plunged into the unknown. They must have suffered trepidation and fear, although there is no record of their experience. Enduring unknown misadventures, they traveled by night into Pennsylvania—first to Gettysburg, then Harrisburg, Reading and, finally, Philadelphia. The transformation from enslaved men to freedom seekers was marked by the change of names—in Basil's case, from Ephraim Costly to Basil Dorsey, and in his brothers' cases, to William, Charles and Thomas Dorsey.

In Philadelphia, the Dorsey brothers somehow connected with Robert Purvis. Purvis was an African American dedicated to fighting slavery and wealthy enough to be independent. He would become one of the founders of the Philadelphia Anti-Slavery Society in May 1836, the first Black member of the Pennsylvania Abolition Society and the founder of the Philadelphia Vigilant Committee in August 1837.

Dorsey's story seems to revolve around meeting Purvis, perhaps because Purvis's interviews with R.C. Smedley and Edward Magill are the main primary sources about Dorsey. Purvis helped Dorsey to deal with seizure and arrest under the first Fugitive Slave Act of 1793. Purvis's aid led to Dorsey's eventual reunion with his wife after his escape and before his triumph at his 1837 Doylestown trial. Purvis introduced Dorsey to Joshua Leavitt, who directed Dorsey to his ultimate home in Florence, Massachusetts.

The meeting with Purvis was decisive for three of the Dorsey brothers. Purvis would use his familial and abolitionist networks on their behalf. Purvis started by finding employment for Basil, William and Charles in Bucks County, Pennsylvania. Thomas chose to stay in Philadelphia. Purvis employed Basil at his farm in Byberry, while the other two brothers worked with nearby farmers.

It was through Purvis that Louisa rejoined Basil. By prior plan, she traveled from Maryland to Purvis in Philadelphia in the company of her

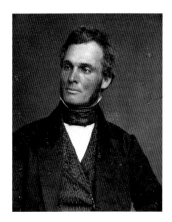

A dashing and handsome Robert Purvis was included in the daguerreotype of the Philadelphia Vigilance Committee, 1850–59. *Arts Department, Boston Public Library.*

free brother-in-law, whose name is unknown. Happily, by then, Louisa had managed to achieve her freedom and came accompanied by their new baby, John Richard, as well as their older daughter, Eliza.

For a year or two, the Dorsey brothers calmly lived a free life. In the summer of 1837, their luck changed. Louisa's brother-in-law became jealous and betrayed their location to Sollers and his slave catchers, James Wagner and Daniel Sweadner. In July, Wagner and Sweadner caught and arrested Thomas in Philadelphia, taking him to a slave trader's jail in Baltimore. Before Thomas could be sold south to New Orleans, however, abolitionist allies saved him by purchasing his freedom.

That left the other three Dorsey brothers in a tense situation, but Purvis reacted quickly. Having just returned home from Philadelphia, Purvis was eating his dinner when he heard news of Basil's capture. The slave catchers had found Basil plowing and overpowered and handcuffed him. They had come prepared with warrants from Judge John Fox of Doylestown and with a constable from nearby Bristol to execute them. They arrested Basil and put him in the jail in Bristol. Basil's warrant identified him as "Ephraim," about "twenty six or seven years old, about five feet seven or nine inches high, stout made and of yellow complexion."

Purvis rushed to Bristol just as the constable was jailing Basil. First, Purvis craftily made a speech to the gathering crowd to arouse public sympathy. He then persuaded Sollers, Basil's owner, to go together with him to Judge Fox in Doylestown the following morning.

Purvis could then worry about the other two Dorsey brothers. Purvis hurried home to discover them already nearby. Purvis equipped Charles with a loaded gun. Seeing the gun, the slave catchers promptly left. Purvis then used the cover of night to drive Charles and William to his brother Joseph's farm. Purvis knew he could rely on Joseph to take the brothers forty miles away to a sympathizer located in New Jersey. From there, one Dorsey brother was able to travel to Canada, and the other apparently stayed in New York.

The next day dawned. The slave catchers ignored their agreement to meet Purvis in Bristol and instead left early. They planned to meet illicitly with Judge Fox to resolve Dorsey's custody in their favor. Dorsey got word to Purvis only by quick thinking. He yelled a message to a woman along the way, who relayed it to Purvis. Purvis relied on a fast horse to catch up to the kidnappers where they were breakfasting near Doylestown. Their stop gave Purvis an opportunity to tell William H. Johnson, another Underground Railroad agent in Bucks County, to spread the word to antislavery sympathizers. Purvis still arrived in Doylestown well ahead of the group with Dorsey. As the slave catchers were taking him to jail, Dorsey held up his manacles, managing to shame the slave catchers in front of the antislavery crowd.

The slave catchers were foiled. Purvis had had enough time to hire a local lawyer named Thomas Ross and to arrange for the arrival of Dorsey's wife and children. Facing Judge Fox, Ross argued to postpone the case in the interests of a proper defense. Dorsey was desperate enough to perjure himself by saying he had left his (nonexistent) free papers in Columbia, Pennsylvania. The piteous spectacle of the disheartened prisoner and his crying family swayed the judge. The judge delayed the trial for two weeks.

Dorsey passed the two weeks manacled in the Doylestown jail. According to a writ of habeas corpus, the judge was not to decide whether Dorsey could be discharged until August. Purvis, meanwhile, resorted to renowned lawyer David Paul Brown. Brown was not just any White lawyer—he was a respected criminal lawyer with a record of helping enslaved African Americans pro bono.

Sollers arrived with his witnesses, his bill of sale for "Ephraim" (now Basil Dorsey) and his own backup plan. He offered Dorsey's legal freedom for $500. Dorsey begged Purvis to buy his freedom, until Sollers greedily decided to increase his price to $800 and then to $1,000. Enough was enough. Dramatically, Dorsey proclaimed: "No more offers, if the decision goes against me, I will cut my throat in the Court House. I will not go back to slavery." Thankfully, Dorsey did not have to go to that extreme.

In case the court's decision should favor the slave owner, Purvis had secretly mobilized the local African American community to plan a rescue. Before Sollers could take Dorsey back to slavery in Maryland, a group stationed at one of the roads leading out of town would stop him.

On the day of the trial, despite the ongoing wheat harvest, the courtroom was full of free African Americans, as well as antislavery Whites. Sollers had only been able to find an inexperienced lawyer willing to represent him. That lawyer was intimidated and befuddled by David Paul Brown. Brown caught the court's attention with his dramatic flair and successfully raised the need for properly certified proof of the legality of slavery in Maryland, the state of the slaveholder. As it had never occurred to him that he would need it, Sollers's lawyer could not produce this certified copy. Dorsey's lawyers triumphed by a technicality. Judge John Fox discharged Dorsey on August 1, 1837.

After the discharge, the judge instructed Sollers to get a new warrant from someone else if the slave owner wished to persist with Dorsey's arrest.

Meanwhile, Dorsey remained in the courtroom, stunned by the verdict, and Purvis had to lead him out, followed by joyful onlookers. Just as Purvis and Dorsey were preparing to leave, the Sollers party returned in time to flourish the warrant and try to stop Purvis's buggy from leaving. Purvis used a flick of his whip to get the horse to rear and run. A protective, cheering crowd ushered Dorsey and Purvis out of town. As observer "W.H.J." (perhaps William H. Johnson) noted: "[Dorsey] soon felt that he breathed the air of freedom."

Purvis rushed Dorsey twenty-six miles to the Philadelphia house of yet another sympathetic relative—Purvis's mother, Harriet Judah. From there, Purvis accompanied him to New York. In New York City, Dorsey met two members of the staff of the abolitionist paper *The Emancipator* through an introduction from Purvis. The help of these men shaped Dorsey's future. They were David Ruggles, secretary of the New York Committee of Vigilance (founded in 1835), and editor Joshua Leavitt, an American Congregationalist minister who was a leader in the American and New York Anti-Slavery Societies (both founded in 1833).

These connections launched Dorsey on a second journey to freedom, this time in Massachusetts. He left behind everything but his wife and children. His brother Charles would only join him in Massachusetts for the two years before Charles died in 1852.

During this second journey to freedom, Dorsey relied on his courage and determination and on his Leavitt ties. Joshua Leavitt directed Dorsey from New York to Northampton, Massachusetts, where Leavitt had family. In Northampton, Dorsey did not stay long with Haynes K. Starkweather, Dorsey's local host. Captain Samuel Parsons, an Underground Railroad operative, transported Dorsey to Charlemont to the care of Joshua Leavitt's brothers—abolitionist Roger Hooker Leavitt and Underground Railroad activist Hart Leavitt. Starting in 1837 or 1838, Dorsey and his family would live with the Roger Hooker Leavitts for about five years.

While in Charlemont, tragedy struck the Dorseys. Louisa Dorsey died a few months after the birth of a son named Charles Robert in 1838. Needing a change, in January 1844, Dorsey and his three children moved to a unique area of Northampton. They would root themselves in Bensonville. Dorsey and his children probably lived with the founder of the Northampton Association of Education and Industry (NAEI), George W. Benson. Account books for 1843–47 show that Dorsey shopped at the NAEI store.

By allying themselves with Northampton Association of Education and Industry members, the Dorseys found a sympathetic and welcoming community of reformers. NAEI had been founded in 1842 in the fashion of other New England utopian communities. NAEI embraced religious, racial and gender equality, as well as abolition and communal living. NAEI owned farmland and a cooperative silk mill—silk because of an opportunity in the local silk industry. In addition to White founders George Benson, Samuel Hill and James Stetson, NAEI came to include African American activists David Ruggles and Sojourner Truth. NAEI's link to antislavery was not surprising, since a frequent visitor was Benson's brother-in-law William Lloyd Garrison, the famed editor of the abolitionist newspaper *The Liberator*.

The Northampton Association of Education and Industry became economically distressed. Abolitionist capitalists bought the silk mill in 1846 and converted the mill to use slave-grown cotton to produce textiles. Like Benson, J.P. Williston, the next president of the mill, proved to be what the *Hampshire Gazette* called "a firm and faithful friend" to Dorsey and other African Americans. Williston continued hiring freedom seekers. In 1850, of Florence's six hundred residents, about 10 percent were African American.

Although the Northampton Association of Education and Industry only existed for four and a half years, it created the opportunity for Dorsey to hold a steady job, first as a teamster and then as a jobber for the cotton mill. As a teamster, Dorsey transported the bales of cotton to the mill and the cotton cloth back to the railroad in Northampton. Once a jobber, he traveled more widely.

In 1849, Dorsey used his wages to buy a house lot in the factory village from Williston. By the time of the census of 1850, Dorsey was living in a vernacular Greek Revival–style house built on the lot. Dorsey's household included not only his second wife, Cynthia Jones (a local woman of nineteen), and their baby but also the children from his first marriage: two sons and the family of his eldest child, Eliza.

Nonotuck Street, where Dorsey's house was located, was home to a total of thirty-five African Americans in 1850, presumably including freedom seekers. A few years earlier, an NAEI schoolteacher, Sophia Foord, had written to a friend, Robert Adams, on May 8, 1843, about the local community's embrace of freedom seekers:

> *This is becoming, or has already become, quite a depot for fugitives—one left here on Thursday & another arrived the day following who will probably tarry a short time.*

J.P. Williston's December 18, 1850 letter to his mentor Ichabod S. Spencer described the lives of the freedom seekers:

Basil Dorsey's first house on Nonotuck Road in Florence is now called the Dorsey-Jones House. *David Ruggles Center.*

> *They came to me destitute of everything. They have now good comfortable houses of their own, with gardens, poultry, swine, decent clothing, furniture, etc.…Their children were ignorant of letters when they came, now they have the rudiments of a good common education, can read, write & cypher.*

Dorsey's trajectory was typical. By the time Purvis visited Dorsey after the Civil War, chronicler Magill said Purvis found Dorsey to be "a well-to-do citizen, with an interesting wife and number of children, all of whom had received or were receiving a good education." As Roger Hart Leavitt's niece later recalled, Dorsey himself had learned "his letters, and to read some" from her as a young girl.

The Dorseys did not attain this happy situation automatically. It was threatened by the passage of the 1850 Fugitive Slave Act. Dorsey and nine other freedom seekers turned to the community. On October 15, 1850, they signed and published a call for a meeting protesting the new law. The signers sought local protection from a return to "a tyranny far worse than death." In the call, the freedom seekers proclaimed they were "guilty of no crime, save their love

To the Citizens of Northampton.

The undersigned, fugitives from Southern Slavery, respectfully call your attention to the law recently enacted by the Congress of the United States, and approved by the President, which requires the officers of Government, aided and assisted by all good citizens, to seize upon, and convey back those persons guilty of no crime, save their love of liberty, to a state of bondage worse than that existing in any part of the known world, denying its victims all social, political, and religious rights, reducing them to chattelism, and articles of merchandise, mercilessly separating families, and refusing them the Bible, and the attainment of all knowledge.

Aided and directed by a kind Providence we have effected our escape from this deplorable servitude and fled to Massachusetts for an asylum and refuge, confidently believing she would not betray the wanderer, nor deliver up the oppressed.

For our orderly, peaceful, and quiet behavior in our adopted State, we fearlessly challenge investigation; by our industry and sobriety we have many of us accumulated property, and under the free, fostering, and liberal policy of this noble commonwealth, have become citizens, and eligible to any office in the gift of the people. The enactment of this cruel and unrighteous law has thrown us into a state of alarm and consternation, for fear we may be torn from our families and friends and again doomed to a tyranny far worse than death.

We therefore respectfully invite the inhabitants of the town of Northampton, irrespective of party, or sect, to assemble in public meeting in the Town Hall, on Wednesday eve, the 23d inst., at 6 1-2 o'clock, to express their opinions and adopt such measures as they may deem proper to prevent Massachusetts from being made slave hunting ground,—the purity of the Judiciary from being soiled by legal bribes, and the public Treasury from being robbed to perpetrate these gross and enormous wrongs.

BASIL DORSEY,	JOHN WILLIAMS,
WM. C. RANDELL,	LEWIS FRENCH,
JOSEPH WILSON,	WM. HENRY BOYER,
GEORGE WRIGHT,	HENRY ANTHONY,
LOSENBERRY,	WM. WRIGHT.

Dorsey was the first name on this call for a meeting to protest the 1850 Fugitive Slave Act, published in the *Northampton Courier*. *David Ruggles Center*.

of liberty" and had "by [their] industry and sobriety" become property owners. They proudly claimed the status of citizens of the Commonwealth of Massachusetts. They invited other city residents to join them in preventing Massachusetts from becoming a "slave hunting ground."

At the meeting held on October 23, 1850, the Northampton Town Hall was reported to be "well filled." Speakers tried to reassure the alarmed freedom seekers. C.P. Huntington, a lawyer and abolitionist, was sanguine enough to assert that "principles of Freedom have sufficient root in the soil, the institutions and laws of Massachusetts, and in the souls of her citizens" to protect all. Another speaker, the Reverend John Newton Mars, was a Methodist preacher based in Springfield. Mars had become dedicated to antislavery activity because of his parents' enslavement before his birth in freedom. Mars flourished a copy of the bill "dressed" in mourning black and proclaimed a welcome to "fugitives" rather than slave catchers. Mars, too, advised freedom seekers to stay despite the new law.

Freedom seekers themselves were not so sure about staying. For example, the Coopers and the Willsons left Bensonville for Canada. With the support of his community, however, Dorsey felt safe enough to stay even though he hauled loads as far away as Providence and Boston. The reputation Dorsey had made for himself inspired local benefactors in Northampton and Florence to buy his freedom from Sollers. They did so despite their qualms about paying money for what they considered to be given by God. Even though Dorsey had lived in freedom for fifteen years, he still needed the legal title that Sollers transferred to Dorsey's agent in May 1851. Lawyer George Griscom of Philadelphia paid $150, of which Dorsey himself contributed $50. After the registration of the bill of sale, Griscom promptly manumitted Dorsey.

VIEW OF THE TOWN HALL, NORTHAMPTON, MASSACHUSETTS.

Northampton City Hall was the site of the fugitive slave law protest meeting. *Courtesy Historic Northampton.*

That redemption of his freedom enabled Dorsey to stay in Bensonville (renamed Florence in 1852) until his death in 1872 at age sixty-two. An 1867 *Hampshire Gazette* article celebrated him as someone who had "always been industrious, and a hard-worker." Elizabeth Powell Bond's eulogy praised his "strength and faithfulness." Dorsey left his well-earned legacy of community standing to his fourteen children.

Robert Purvis was deeply moved by Dorsey's legal battle, which he called "the most interesting case of my long and eventful life." Dorsey's trial in Doylestown made clear to Purvis the need for a new organization, the Vigilant Association of Philadelphia, comparable to the organization already existing in New York City. In the same month as the trial, August 1837, Purvis gathered other African American abolitionists to establish financial support for freedom seekers. By 1839, the organization was providing room and board, clothing and medical care, legal counsel and transportation to freedom seekers, after first taking the precaution of screening for imposters. The Vigilant Association lasted until a major race riot in Philadelphia in 1842. An effective replacement would only emerge in 1852 as a response to the impact of the Fugitive Slave Act of 1850.

Chapter 3

CROSSING THE WIDE WATERS

JOHN THOMPSON (SOUTHERN MARYLAND), 1835

Like many nineteenth-century African Americans, John Thompson had quite a story to tell, despite the fact that his life was cut short at forty-seven. John Thompson was a successful freedom seeker from southern Maryland. After escaping by way of Washington, D.C., Pennsylvania and New York City, John Thompson fled to New Bedford, a whaling port in Massachusetts. In 1842, he signed onto the ship *Milwood* under Captain Aaron C. Luce. From 1842 to 1844, he went around the world hunting whales. By constant travel, he was protected from pursuit by slave catchers.

John Thompson's story was preserved by publication in 1856 as *The Life of John Thompson, a Fugitive Slave*. Thompson took advantage of the popularity of a new type of American autobiography called a "slave narrative." His book was one among several such slave narratives published in Worcester, Massachusetts, an abolitionist hot spot. Abolitionists there encouraged freedom seekers to tell their enthralling stories in order to create broader familiarity with the brutal institution of slavery.

At the time of the publication of *The Life of John Thompson, a Fugitive Slave*, John Thompson was practicing the trade of whitewasher in Worcester, Massachusetts. His occupation in 1859, the year he died, was "book agent," explaining Thompson's personal motive in publishing the book. Apparently, he was no longer able to do the strenuous work of whitewashing. He turned to selling his book to support himself and his family while suffering from ultimately fatal consumption.

Thompson undoubtedly did not want to confess a profit motive. In his preface, he justified publication of his story by saying that there were "scarcely any [other narratives] from Maryland." He ignored two widely sold slave narratives by famed Maryland freedom seekers: *The Narrative of the Life of Frederick Douglass* by Frederick Douglass (1845) and *The Fugitive Blacksmith* (1849) by James W.C. Pennington.

Today, Thompson's book is considered unique for his successful manner of escape and his literary approach. To a nineteenth-century reader, what stood out was the likelihood that Thompson, rather than an abolitionist editor, was the author. Thompson defied the stereotype of the uneducated, enslaved African American. His book is studded with biblical references and lines from hymns. He quotes poetry. He ends with what amounts to a sermon, using a sailing voyage as a metaphor for a Christian's life.

When noting publication of Thompson's book, on August 22, 1856, the abolitionist newspaper *The Liberator* called attention not to the whaling voyage he made but to the author's "education through stealth." During enslavement, Thompson learned from secret teachers like an orphan he escorted to school, a fellow bondsman and an Englishman. Thompson said he came to love liberty through reading a scrap from a speech by John Quincy Adams. During Thompson's early years of freedom, he continued learning at an evening school in Philadelphia. Thompson called his education "one of my greatest blessings." Thompson was proud that he "spared no exertions to learn to read and write," and judged that he succeeded "tolerably well."

Nineteenth-century readers expected the author of a slave narrative to bring plantation slavery to life in all its cruelty. Thompson was careful to do so, including examples from Maryland that would have also been typical of the brutality of the Deep South. Thompson omitted no horrors. He included details of whippings, which more than once continued "until the blood stood in puddles." He described the meager and limited diet, the small ration of clothing and the extended work hours. Thompson elaborated on the unrelenting and arbitrary punishments, sexual exploitation, separation through sale and restrictions on religious practice. He even showed how his owner and her son passed on such cruel behavior to a child by lavishing praise on him for whipping enslaved children.

Thompson used stereotypical characters: cruel owners and overseers, slave traders and martyred bondsmen. However, he went beyond most other authors of slave narratives by creating extended scenarios. For example, he chose an early traumatic memory: his family's final goodbye to his elder sister as she awaited shipment to Alabama for public auction. All the sisters and brothers went with their mother. Thompson described the slave trader's yard with its rattling of chains as "a hell upon earth, emblematic of that dreadful dungeon [hell] where the wicked are kept." There were tears and embraces by family members as the sun slowly set, bringing the time to part. His sister's last statement was intended to move his readers: "If we are faithful, we shall meet again where partings are no more [in heaven]."

For Thompson, an important theme was the indomitable spirit of himself and his fellow bondsmen. He did not portray the enslaved as suffering passively. He was explicit: "There are many there [in the South] who would rather be shot than whipped by any man." He began with himself. Thompson attacked an overseer rather than receive unjust punishment. In another instance, Thompson resolved to kill if beaten again by his employer.

In his narrative, Thompson provided those resisting with a degree of triumph, albeit with certain costs. Thompson told the story of "resolute and brave" Ben, who resisted the overseer's blows and fought back. Although Ben received a severe whipping, his owner did not confront or sell him. One of John Thompson's sisters was a beautiful and virtuous housemaid. She managed to avoid her owner's lecherous advances through escape. This escape, however, came at the expense of the husband and child she was forced to abandon.

When Thompson reached the story of his own escape, he shifted from a catalogue of suffering and limited resistance. Thompson emphasized God's role, because of his own growing faith as well as religion's appeal to his audience. Thompson portrayed God as the instigator of his escape and his protector during his pursuit by slave catchers. As Thompson wrote of the local enslaved population in general, his own conversion to Methodism "brought glad tidings to the poor bondsman…and opened the prison doors to them that were bound."

The Life of John Thompson, a Fugitive Slave began, typically, with the story of life in slavery. When it came to more than anecdotes and a list of cruelties, however, Thompson was unusually vague about details. He may have invented his owners' surname. He neither specified the county where he was born in 1812 nor where he grew up. He wrote only that he came from Maryland's tobacco country and was hired out near Washington, D.C., and Prince George's County. Thompson explained that he was evasive because of fear for himself and for "my sister, whose name I must not mention, as she is now in the North, and like myself, not out of danger."

Tobacco was the cash crop in southern Maryland, where Thompson grew up. *Library of Congress.*

Thompson wrote that he grew up on the plantation of James H. Wagar, who had 50 bondsmen of his own and was in charge of another 150 of his mother's. Thompson's parents and their children (two girls and five boys) belonged to James's mother, only identified as "Mrs. Wagar."

Under James Wagar, Thompson's father, Cyrus, and his mother were field hands, but his second sister worked in the Big House as a "house girl" (housemaid). For three years, although living away from his parents, youthful John was proud to enjoy a similar status as body servant for James Wagar's son, also named John. As a house servant, John Thompson could eat and dress better than a field hand and could snatch the chance to learn to read and write.

Most of Thompson's family continued in Mrs. Wagar's possession until she died in October 1822. As was often the case, Mrs. Wagar's death meant division of her belongings, including her enslaved African Americans. Thompson explained that George Thomas was married to "my old Mistress' daughter," so in 1823, Thomas took over management of Thompson and his family, "who fell to him in right of his wife."

Valued as hard workers, Thompson's mother rose to cook and his father and brother to overseers. These positions gave his family some protection through appeal to Richard Thomas, a brother of George, and to John Thompson's owner, Elizabeth, a granddaughter of Mrs. Wagar.

According to Thompson, George Thomas was "a man of wealth, his farm consisting of about one thousand acres of land, well stocked with slaves." Possibly the farm was too well stocked, since George Thomas started Thompson on a trajectory of being hired out or sold to a succession of plantation and farm owners. Thompson passed from one to another, rarely improving his circumstances of long days, a meager diet, scanty clothing and, of course, bloody whippings.

Thompson's placements included a gambler, a hypocritical Catholic, a dissipated and impoverished planter and a farmer who owned only one bondsman and hired the rest. The best of the lot, a Mr. Horken, fed the enslaved workers poorly but was a "tolerably good man, so far as whipping was concerned." Under each, Thompson faced punishment for trivial or nonexistent offenses. His recourse was temporary escape to the woods, appeal to his owner, physical resistance or contemplation of permanent disappearance. Thompson was hesitant to escape because he knew of freedom seekers who were caught and, after a whipping, sold south. However, he came to bitterly regret having distrusted God to the extent that he neglected an opportunity to join a party of freedom seekers, with a stronger faith in God than his, who arrived safely in Canada.

Finally, Thompson had to escape because he had earlier unwittingly revealed his literacy. Thompson had been in the habit of handwriting passes to enable him to leave the plantation. One day, he confused a forged pass in his pocket with a message intended for delivery. His literacy became public knowledge.

An escape occurred where Thompson had formerly worked. Rumors began flying that Thompson was writing passes and encouraging escapes. Thompson was shocked to hear that an informer he did not know was claiming that Thompson was tempting him to run away. It was true that Thompson was considering escape because his owner's brother had permission to move him to Mississippi. Thompson had believed his intention to be known only to the unidentified friend who would accompany him.

At the end of one of Thompson's Sundays off, constables awaited him because three freedom seekers had been caught, allegedly with plans to accompany him. That afternoon, though, Thompson felt himself repeatedly blocked from returning to his employer's estate as usual. He felt compelled to hide overnight in the woods. In the morning, his uncle Harry informed Thompson of a $300 reward for his capture.

Thompson recognized God's intervention to prevent his capture. In return for a solemn promise of service to God, he perceived a thunderous voice promising support, come what may. He realized that now, with God's support, he should flee. During what would be his last visit with his mother, he said nothing of his plans, because she was already heartbroken about the imminent consequences of the accusations against him. Although his heart was pierced by the prospect that he might never see his mother again, upon leaving her, he immediately stopped to praise God for His protection so far.

After a week hiding in the woods, Thompson's only recourse was to turn to the friend with whom he had planned to escape. As his friend was coachman for his owner, he had a room above the kitchen to himself. Thompson hid there unnoticed. Meanwhile, his friend, who knew the escape routes, wavered about his promise. When he finally decided to flee, they left that very evening. After walking a few miles, they saw a group of horses grazing nearby. They took advantage of two to spend the night riding at full speed, covering perhaps forty miles.

Thompson relied on the ultimate Underground Railroad operative, the "Great Conductor." Thompson and his companion learned to trust fellow men and women of God. Along the way, enslaved and free African Americans helped them with directions, guides, food and drink and spiritual sustenance. For example, in Washington, D.C., Thompson happened to meet a trustworthy fellow Christian raised on his home farm. This man directed the two freedom seekers to the house of a free woman who listened to their story, prayed with them, fed them and indicated the dangerous spots on their projected route.

Despite their trust in the "Great Conductor," the freedom seekers' trip was marked by fear. Many pursuers sought to earn the $300 reward for Thompson's capture—workmen at a bridge, several Irish quarrymen, two young boys, two overly interested horsemen and a large group near Rockville. The freedom seekers escaped them all and passed Rockville. On the outskirts of Frederick, the freedom seekers made use of Thompson's literacy. He related that they "pulled down a guideboard [road sign]" to determine the road to follow. The two freedom seekers avoided Baltimore and the Susquehanna River as they headed for the Pennsylvania border.

Thompson and his companion suffered hunger, exhaustion and swollen feet. To avoid pursuit, they cut through fields and swamps. The two sheltered in unexpected places—not only under a fallen tree or in a rye field but also among bondsmen at a plantation, among a group of churchgoers and with a drunken freeman in his lean-to in the woods.

Just before reaching the Pennsylvania border, the two companions had to maneuver past a man with dogs and sneak by a slave trader's house. The last obstacle between them and the state line was a professional slave catcher and his dogs. They successfully reached the Baltimore Turnpike and so passed over the Pennsylvania state line.

In Pennsylvania, the freedom seekers felt safe, but they learned that they were wrong. To begin with, near York, a "Dutchman" (German) chased them. At Columbia, they heard word of slave catchers already after others in flight, so they didn't stop to look for work. Ten miles further along, they "reached the house of an elderly Quaker" who found them jobs. For six months, Thompson found joy in the "reflection that I was working for myself."

When African Americans living around them began to move away to avoid slave hunters, Thompson and his friend decided they needed to flee to Philadelphia. To their dismay, Philadelphia was not necessarily safe either, despite being a Quaker stronghold. Thompson wrote that his friend met but ignored "a lady" who knew him and thought he saw "his old master… peering into the face of every colored man who happened to pass." Soon, Thompson's friend married and fled to Massachusetts.

Left alone, Thompson made poor choices in friends until he turned to religion again. Opening the Bible, he came upon a verse that led him to attend the Methodist Conference revival at the "Bethel Church" (Mother Bethel African Methodist Episcopal Church). While attending, he was quite ill, but a hymn calling for a return to God spoke directly to him, as did the unforgettable preacher from Baltimore. Thompson became a member of the church that very night.

Thompson met his future wife, married and became a father. He worked as a waiter and assisted brickmasons. When there were arrests and seizures of other freedom seekers, Thompson realized he was still not secure. The slave

Mother Bethel African Methodist Episcopal Church in Philadelphia was founded in 1794. *Special Collections Research Center, Temple University Libraries, Philadelphia.*

Between 1740 and 1865, "sailor" was an important occupation for Blacks. *Collection of the Smithsonian National Museum of African American History and Culture.*

narrative jumps to Thompson's unusual solution: the ocean as an ultimate refuge. He decided to become a "Black Jack," as African American sailors were called. Thompson could pass as one of the free Black seamen sailing the world.

The regimen on board a ship offered a rough equality. Black sailors shared in all work on board, whether or not they were assigned to the privileged positions of cook or steward. All sailors were subject to the same punishments. On the other hand, the captain could be arbitrary and the White seamen racist. Compared to slavery, nonetheless, seamen could learn skills, assert masculinity and obtain information freely. Though dangerous, the sea provided an occupation, with Seamen's Protection Papers African Americans could carry proudly.

After Thompson fled Philadelphia, he could not find a berth at his first stop, New York City. He continued on to New Bedford, Massachusetts, for free, having made contact with an agent representing that city's merchants. Whale oil was a major source of lighting in the nineteenth century, and New Bedford was a center for whalers bringing back the oil. The whaling ships always needed hands and were likely to take those without experience.

Black Jacks on whaling ships endured hard and dangerous work and a poor diet, harsh punishments and cramped living conditions. The choice, however, was voluntary. Under the lay system, any profits from the voyage were shared by all according to the fraction agreed upon when signing up. At the end of the voyage, sailors were paid, after expenses incurred for clothes or sundries were deducted. Many shipped out for only one whaling trip, for whatever reason. Examples of freedom seekers who became whaling men are Anthony Allen (in 1807), who ended up in Hawaii, and Joseph Jacobs (in 1846), who ended up in Australia.

When Thompson arrived in New Bedford, he arranged for a seaman's certificate, prudently putting Adams County, Pennsylvania, as his home.

Left: John Thompson identified a home in a free state on the *Milwood* crew list on June 24, 1842. *New Bedford Port Society, New Bedford, MA.*

Below: In the background, a whaling ship sails outward bound from New Bedford, passing Martha's Vineyard. *Smithsonian American Art Museum, museum purchase.*

An entire whale stamped in the logbook meant a catch, while a tail meant a fruitless chase. *Courtesy of the New Bedford Whaling Museum.*

Given the need for sailors, recruiters were not fussy about the prior history of prospective crew members. Thompson boldly presented himself as a candidate for steward on the *Milwood*. The surviving crew list confirms his success. When seasickness made his inexperience obvious, he confessed to the captain that he was a freedom seeker. The captain took pity on him and secretly gave him cooking lessons. Gradually, Thompson gained the captain's goodwill and respect and so was protected from the ill will of the mate.

The *Milwood* roamed the whaling grounds of the Atlantic, Indian and Pacific Oceans. During the two-year voyage, Thompson became well acquainted with whaling and the raging sea. Judging by the ship's logbook, kept by the first mate, Thompson's world constricted to the ship and its crew and his concerns to whales, weather, wind, sky and encounters with other New England ships, which took news home.

Needing barrels of whale oil to make a profit, the captain and crew were ever on the lookout for whales, in this case for right whales. If they sighted a right whale, a "blackfish" (pilot whale) or a sperm whale, weather permitting, the crew lowered the smaller boats, with six sailors each in chase. If not disappointed, the crew succeeded in a "strike" and a killing.

There was, however, much that could go wrong. A line attached to the whale could snap. The struggles of a giant whale could injure a man or destroy a whale boat. A dead whale might sink to the bottom of the sea.

If they were lucky, the crew was able to tow and fasten the dead whale alongside the *Milwood*. The industrial side of the operation, "cutting in," could begin. The crew butchered the whale, boiled the fat down into oil and scraped the "bones" (baleen) in order to sell them to make buggy whips, parasols and hoop skirts.

Days could pass without sighting land. Days in port were rare and valued. The ship stopped in the Azores, the Cape Verde Islands, Cape Town, Madagascar, New Zealand and St. Helena Island and rounded Cape Horn. Long stops were only made in South Africa, Madagascar and St. Helena. Climate varied, and the crew sighted icebergs more than once. Through his travels, Thompson became more cosmopolitan, becoming exposed, for example, to Islam.

Thompson marveled at the size and behavior of the great mammal, gaining respect for "the whale…a monster, terrible in his fury, but harmless when left alone." Thompson had ample opportunity to observe the ways of whaling, from hunt to catch to processing. The bark caught over thirty-one whales and brought back to New Bedford 12,000 pounds of baleen and

1,700 barrels of right whale oil, as well as 150 more barrels of oil from the highly prized sperm whale.

Thompson's faith was influenced by his experience at sea. He found that his faith turned out to be an advantage, as it was for Jonah in the Bible. The *Milwood* was involved in several terrible storms, and the captain and the crew noticed that Thompson's prayers were followed by deliverance. His prayers also preceded the successful capture of whales. Thompson grew to like the metaphor of the soul as a ship like the one on which he lived for two years. In the last chapter of his narrative, he elaborated on it: "For nothing so much resembles the passage of a Christian from earth to glory, as a gallant ship under full sail for some distant port."

Only when Thompson felt the trail of his escape was cold was he willing to return to his family, whom he had left in Philadelphia. According to the United States Census, in 1850, he was in Philadelphia with his wife, Rosetta; their baby, Cyrus; and their son Zoriosta, age three. Thompson is recorded as a waiter, age thirty-eight. In 1855, the state census documented his presence in Worcester with his wife, Rosetta, and son William H.E., age eight. Nowhere is there a record of the fifteen years of freedom following his voyage. Thompson did not explain to the public how or why the family ended up in Worcester, Massachusetts, nor how he struggled with consumption until his death. His death certificate listed him as John W. Thompson, born in Maryland about 1812, son of Cyrus Thompson, and age forty-seven upon his death in Worcester on October 3, 1859.

Thompson's slave narrative is basically a discussion of his religious development. Nonetheless, Thompson's description of life on a whaling ship is a rare freedom seeker's version of two other books well known in Thompson's time. Richard Henry Dana Jr. wrote *Two Years before the Mast* (1840), the seafaring adventure of a Harvard graduate. Herman Melville crafted *Moby-Dick* (1851), an encyclopedic masterpiece in which whaling is central. Slave narratives were and are read with great interest, but those with a special lagniappe of adventure—whether a whaling voyage or the California Gold Rush—have a special appeal.

James Watkins (Baltimore County), 1844

On the Eastern Seaboard, the last resort for desperate freedom seekers was crossing the wide Atlantic. Upholding the torch of liberty, Britain welcomed exiles who made freedom their cause. Britain had eliminated slavery in the empire by 1834. The number of African Americans in Britain multiplied after the Fugitive Slave Act of 1850. Like more famous freedom seekers Frederick Douglass, James W.C. Pennington and Ellen and William Craft, James Watkins fled to Britain in order to escape pursuers.

Britons from all classes and regions showed great curiosity about American slavery. The challenge of the freedom seekers was to court the British public on behalf of the enslaved African Americans. They appealed to British moral integrity and Christianity. If Britons lionized freedom seekers, they were validating African Americans' humanity as fellow Christians and equals. They were accepting former "slaves" as intelligent, moral and feeling human beings, regardless of race.

In writing slave narratives and speaking publicly, African American abolitionists intended to bring to life what James Watkins called the "accursed system of human suffering, degradation, and torture—slavery!" Philosophical arguments were all very well, but when one American reviewer noted that slave narratives "go right to the hearts of men," he could have been speaking of lectures as well.

James Watkins from Baltimore County was one of those freedom seekers who brought the situation of enslaved African Americans to life for Britons through his lectures and the publication of his life story. Watkins did not try to compete with the more famous "fugitive slaves" lecturing and raising money in bigger cities. Instead, James Watkins gave his lectures in churches and schools in villages, towns and smaller cities, especially in the Midlands.

Watkins was able to make a living and mold public opinion by capitalizing on his past. Audiences flocked to hear about the depravity of slavery and the thrilling details of Watkins's escape. To enhance his lectures, Watkins learned to use props—a whip and an iron yoke. He also used music—liberty lyrics set to a familiar tune, a freedom song or what Watkins referred to as "one or two of our negro melodies."

In telling his story, Watkins began by distinguishing between what British workingmen called "slavery" under industrialization and chattel "slavery" in the United States. He pointed out that British workers received wages and

Unsuccessful freedom seekers were forced to wear this awkward and heavy contraption with bells as a punishment and a deterrent. *Louisiana State Museum.*

Young Jacob's Choice, a modest home for a prospering nineteenth-century farmer, was on about two hundred acres. *Baltimore County Department of Planning.*

could switch employers or organize to seek an alternative to mistreatment, long hours and low pay. They were not property subject to sale as though they were furniture or livestock. Enslaved African Americans suffered brutal punishments, forced separations of families and oppression by cruel and immoral slave owners.

It was Watkins's duty to educate his audience about the conditions under which an enslaved person lived. He started with his origins in the slave state of Maryland, which he did not differentiate from the generic "South," with its stereotypical large plantations with large numbers of bondsmen.

Watkins grew up on Young Jacob's Choice, the property of Abraham Ensor in Sparks, Baltimore County. At Abraham's death in 1835, his son Luke B. Ensor inherited or purchased James Watkins. Watkins remained on the estate until his successful escape to freedom. Young Jacob's Choice was only twelve miles from the Pennsylvania border. Ironically, while enslaved, Watkins was not aware of how close freedom lay. Once he knew, he did not wish to state it and thereby detract from the power of his testimony against slavery.

James Watkins was born about 1821, but he did not know exactly when, as "slaves know little of dates." He grew up called by the slave names of Sam Berry or Ensor Sam. His enslaved mother was Milcah Berry. His father,

Amos Salisbury, was the overseer. Watkins called him "a cruel and severe disciplinarian" as well as a "clever and shrewd man." He was a White man who had a legal but childless wife in Baltimore. He neither acknowledged his fatherhood of Milcah's children nor spared them from his discipline.

Caring for Baltimore County's wheat, corn, hay and livestock needed limited year-round labor. Although Watkins called where he lived a "plantation," the number of bondsmen owned by Abraham Ensor was more appropriate for a "farm." The 1810 census listed Abraham Ensor with nine bondsmen. By 1840, when Luke Ensor had already inherited the land, he was owner of only three.

Growing up, Watkins advanced through a number of jobs familiar to the rural poor in Britain. For Watkins, this progression constituted a success story—herding cows (till he was nine years old), picking stones from fields and washing wool (till age twelve), doing farm work and serving the ladies in the Big House as a "body slave." The pinnacle was the status of a trusted "market man."

As a market man, James Watkins was privileged to go to Baltimore with a cart and horses to sell produce. Baltimore, Maryland's biggest city and a growing port, was about twenty-two miles away. Trips there broadened Watkins's horizons. His owner let him go where he wished and stay at a tavern. Even as a market man, however, Watkins was still subject to his owner and other White men.

Watkins did not spare details of his suffering. Aside from describing whippings, for the education of his audience, Watkins described the sale of his two sisters, his brother and a cousin in Baltimore, a center of the slave trade. He evoked the deep grief of his mother and aunt over these separations. He brought to life the traumatic farewell of all the family when visiting the slave pen of "Slater" (Hope Slatter) and "Woodfork" (Austin Woolfolk).

With each additional beating, and after the sale of his family members, Watkins told of his increasing desire for freedom. He knew Britons prized that value. He related how, in order to learn details of this mysterious state, he would sneak away for conversation with nearby lime kiln workers. Two Irish men (compatriots of his audience) described a country of freedom that Watkins found hard to imagine.

Punishment and threat of sale were frequent inducements to leave slavery. Watkins was first impelled by a severe punishment for staying out past curfew in Baltimore. He made an attempt at escape when he was age twenty, in about 1841. He headed north toward Canada, oriented by the North Star. Slave catchers with bloodhounds captured him by the third day.

When the slave catchers returned Watkins, the entire Ensor family upbraided him as ungrateful. Then, the overseer gave him a harsh whipping, "the effects of which I feel to this day." For three months, he had to wear an iron yoke with bells to announce his whereabouts. Until Watkins regained his owner's trust, he was shunned. Neighboring slave owners restricted his association with their bondsmen to avoid "contamination." Watkins could not forget the humiliation and the feeling "that slavery was a burden too heavy to be borne."

In 1842 or 1843, an epidemic of cholera made Watkins fear for his sinful life, so he attended a Methodist camp meeting. He was enraptured by his newfound faith and no longer feared beatings or death. Dramatically, his prayers seemed to stay his owner's hand from punishing him for attending the meeting without permission. The conversion strengthened his conviction to be free. Watkins equipped himself with food, money from selling baskets and a stick and knife for self-defense. In May 1844, he reluctantly left his grieving mother behind.

After Watkins's escape, to whet the appetite of slave catchers, his owner advertised:

> *My runaway negro boy, Sambo, bullet head, full eyes, big mouth, flat nose, and a cut over the eye. A reward of 250 dollars will be given to bring him back alive, and 150 dollars if brought back dead. —Luke Ensor.*

When his owner's advertising had the desired effect on slave catchers, Watkins improvised, no doubt to the great interest of his audience. He discouraged bloodhounds by ingeniously using cayenne pepper and snuff. Despite being outnumbered, he ably fought off a party of three eager bounty hunters. He was famished enough to eat pig swill. To avoid pursuit, he jumped into a river and swam across.

From Baltimore County, Watkins headed to the nearest free state and reached York County, Pennsylvania. Watkins's trust in Providence led him to a house of those he recalled as "kind and sympathizing friends." He must have stumbled onto operatives of the Underground Railroad. He recouped his strength there for three days. His hosts hired him a Black guide. Faced with this guide's desertion, Watkins, by chance or by plan, was befriended by another Black man. This second man rescued him by providing breakfast, a boat ride across the Susquehanna River to Columbia and an introduction to the first of a series of Quakers.

One Quaker in particular was famous, Watkins said, for being "ever ready to assist the poor fugitive." At this unnamed man's advice, he gave himself the freedom name James Watkins as both a rebirth and a precaution. The Quaker offered him employment. Watkins thought his escape successful. With a wage and lodging, Watkins "began to think myself a *man*."

Watkins's audience needed to learn that a fleeing bondsman was never secure unless his owner had given up his claim. After a couple of weeks, slave hunters appeared in the area. Watkins's Quaker employer paid for Watkins to stow himself in a baggage car of a train for the sixty miles to Philadelphia. To see him safely there, the Quaker rode along in a passenger car. On arrival, Underground Railroad "friends" welcomed them at the station. When Watkins collapsed because of his perilous exploits, a "friend" sheltered him for three weeks.

When Watkins recovered, an Underground Railroad agent accompanied him to New York City. There, he recalled meeting "a delightful band of philanthropists," whom he praised as "friends of the downtrodden and deeply injured slave." For the first time in his narrative, he identified one of his helpers, the "Rev. Mr. Wright." Reverend Theodore S. Wright was pastor of the First Colored Presbyterian Church, founding member of the American Anti-Slavery Society and head of the New York Vigilance Committee until the year he died.

Still not safe, Watkins stayed only a day and a night in New York. Then, the antislavery activists thought it prudent to send him about 115 miles away to Hartford, Connecticut. Watkins carried a letter of introduction to A.F. Williams, whom Watkins's editor characterized as "one, among a noble band of friends of the slave, who reside in Hartford and the neighborhood." The recipient of the letter, Austin F. Williams of Farmington, could indeed be helpful. He was a founding member of the Connecticut Antislavery Society and heavily involved with assisting the rebellious Africans who hijacked the ship *Amistad*.

Hartford turned out to be a welcoming place. Watkins found a long-lost uncle. Contrary to their owner's lies about the uncle's sale down south, he had safely escaped fourteen years before. Watkins's uncle took him home. The uncle found Watkins a job as a farm laborer for Austin Williams's brother Horace. In the job, Watkins noted, the "time passed sweetly and gave me such an experience of freedom, not from work—but from serfdom, that made me feel glad I had escaped though at such risks."

In Hartford, Watkins met, courted and married a free woman, Mary Wells. Upon their wedding in April 1845, Watkins established a family and a home. Simultaneously, he and his wife established a business of making and selling hominy (a form of corn). Their legal marriage contrasted with the

Left: Reverend Theodore Sedgewick Wright was the son of a Schenectady barber. *Randolph Linsly Simpson African-American Collection. Yale Collection of American Literature, Beineke Rare Book and Manuscript Library.*

Right: Austin F. Williams was a loyal ally of James Watkins when he was in Hartford and in England. *Connecticut Historical Society.*

casual bonds permitted by a slave owner. By 1851, Mary and James had a boy, Simeon, and two girls, Ellen and Mary.

To enlarge his Hartford family, Watkins risked a return to what he called "the tiger's den" (Maryland) in May 1849. Watkins's arrival astonished his mother, who believed him sold south. During their night of reunion, they joyfully recounted, each to the other, what had passed since Watkins escaped. Watkins was disappointed to find that, despite manumission by Ensor, his mother lacked the proof necessary to accompany him. Watkins still yearned to share his newfound freedom. With his savings and the help of friends, within a year, he redeemed his brother Thomas from slavery.

Many Hartford African Americans were literate, having been born in and shaped by New England. Watkins worked to emulate them. Learning his ABCs from the small daughter of his employer, Horace Williams, made Watkins "feel as though I was going to be one of some account in the world." After doing farm work, Watkins found work as a porter and a servant. From employers, Watkins learned more and more of "things belonging to civilized society.… I felt the change from the heathen life I had left." His employer,

Roswell Brown, for example, sat on the city council and directed an insurance company and a bank.

Watkins also had a role model in Reverend James W.C. Pennington. Pennington was a brilliant Yale-educated clergyman and himself a Maryland freedom seeker. He had been attracted to Hartford by the gripping 1840 trial of the African rebels from the *Amistad*.

Pennington was ordained pastor of the Black Congregational church on Talcott Street. He served there from 1840 to 1848, overlapping with Watkins's time in Hartford (about 1845–51). Pennington's growing church offered African Americans opportunities for free speech, antislavery lectures, a school, social activities and the experience of building organizations. Significantly, Pennington made his church and home Underground Railroad stations.

Life in Hartford was as insecure as elsewhere. In succession in the 1830s and 1840s came the arrest of Prudence Crandall for teaching Black children (1832), anti-Black riots (1834, 1835) and the case of Nancy Jackson (1837), a bondswoman brought into Connecticut to live, by which action she should have been freed legally. All sent shock waves through the Hartford African American community.

For the Watkins family, it was the disastrous 1850 Fugitive Slave Law that rocked their world. Despite his wife's pleas to flee, Watkins hesitated to leave home. He was, however, faced with the alternative of a return to slavery's hateful tyranny and moral corruption. He regretfully left his family and the comfort, prosperity and wide circle of friends he enjoyed in Hartford.

In January 1851, equipped with letters of introduction to those he called "philanthropists in the 'old world,'" he fled to New York. There, he hid in a hotel until, with the captain's connivance, he was smuggled onto the ship *Arctic*. Arriving in Liverpool after three weeks spent hiding at sea, Watkins felt overwhelmed by joy. He sang "a song of liberty," shouted and jumped, to the amazement of observers who thought him drunk.

With the help of the recommendations from home and from Pennington (already in Britain), Watkins found a niche as an abolitionist lecturer. He listened to British lecturers and learned skills by necessity, innate ability and practice in small groups. At the urging of a mentor, Reverend Francis Tucker, Watkins launched his speaking career in the industrial city of Manchester, in June 1851.

From the beginning, Watkins's subjects were slavery's horrors, slave trafficking, the incompatibility of Christianity and slavery, the Fugitive Slave Act and his escape. He wrote that he soon found "audiences easily obtainable, when it has been understood that a 'black man was going to

 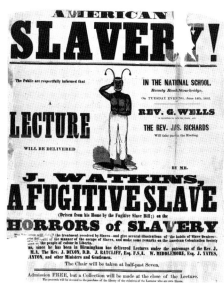

Left: James Watkins would have dressed like a gentleman for his lectures. *Bolton Library and Museum Services, Bolton, United Kingdom.*

Right: This poster advertising a lecture by James Watkins included multiple attention-grabbing details. *Worcester County Council, United Kingdom.*

address them about slavery.'" After all, a Black man was a novelty, especially one who could talk firsthand about twenty years in slavery. In addition, he could offer the opportunity to contribute toward freeing a bondsman.

Watkins's lecture circuit grew so that by August 26, 1865, the *Caledonian Mercury* could claim he had spoken in "the greater part of France and England." He lectured in one thousand sites, since mapped by the British historian Hannah-Rose Murray. The appeals for donations accompanying his lectures yielded him what he called a "comfortable living."

Watkins impressed his audiences. Using skillful marketing, one poster showed him dressed as a gentleman. The *Preston Chronicle*, on August 19, 1854, stated that he "appears to be a very intelligent man, and quote[s] Cowper and other English poets, in support of his arguments for the abolition of slavery." The *Liverpool Mercury*, on July 8, 1858, wrote that, although without what it called education, he had "that erudition, taste, and judgment, those eminent excellences of genius which invigorate the powers of his understanding and animate the faculties of his mind."

Watkins developed the ability, said a Lancaster paper in 1861, to create "a feeling of sympathy…seldom seen equaled in any public meeting." Watkins

Reverend James W.C. Pennington, author of *The Fugitive Blacksmith*, escaped from Rockland in Washington County in 1827. *National Portrait Gallery, Smithsonian Institution.*

knew his audiences. Beyond drawing on their horror and pity, he thrillingly described his progression from ignorance and sin. He emphasized his conversion to Methodism. He contrasted Christian values with the lies, theft and Sabbath work that slaveholders forced on those they enslaved. He concluded with the noxious moral and physical effects that the institution of slavery had on both enslavers and enslaved.

Watkins attacked the notion that bondsmen were inferior and had no feelings. He would write, "We *have* feelings, slaves though we have been." He repeatedly brought up his longing to see the family he had left in slavery and his family in Connecticut. He focused on ties close to everyone's heart—those to a mother, a wife and children, a home. He repeatedly evoked the despair of his mother—over her and her family's enslavement, over the sale of some of her children and over his disclosure of his plan to escape. He made his audience share the happiness of his cozy life in Hartford and his utter joy upon arrival in Liverpool.

Watkins's lectures on his progression from slavery to freedom created enough interest to prompt publication. Although now literate, Watkins was intimidated enough to need help with a book. As his book's preface related, in Bolton, "a Friend indeed," the unidentified H.R., took down the story "as the words dropped from the lips" of Watkins. Then, H.R. arranged the dictation into a narrative autobiography. In February 1852, Kenyon and Abbatt Printers in Bolton published Watkins's book, *Narrative of the Life of James Watkins*.

That same year, Harriet Beecher Stowe published *Uncle Tom's Cabin*, an immense success in the United Kingdom. The freedom seekers' lectures and slave narratives both set the stage for, and benefited from, its sale of over eight million copies in eight months.

Narrative of the Life of James Watkins shared some of Stowe's success and sold nineteen editions. The final edition, in 1860, was printed in Manchester by A. Heywood, who called Watkins "a standing monument of the injustice of American institutions toward his class." In what was now entitled *Struggles for Freedom; or the Life of James Watkins*, the appended list of Watkins's presentations had grown. Added were an update on his life in Birmingham and miscellaneous addenda like a prestigious letter from Lord Denman accepting Watkins's invitation to a meeting. After almost a decade of help, Watkins emphasized his gratitude to the Britons in general and the clergy in particular. He was surer of himself, as shown by his frankness about British racial prejudice. Some embellishments had been added, to be sure, making Young Jacob's Choice a grand plantation (not a farm), where Aunt Comfort cared for eighty or ninety children, not two, and Ensor preached to three to four hundred African Americans. Watkins now had to travel one thousand miles to arrive in Hartford, and he was helped by Red Indians, not only by Quakers.

Over the years, Watkins had prospered in Britain. Austin F. Williams in Hartford negotiated purchase of his freedom from Ensor in 1851, assuring Watkins's legal status. Thanks to appeals for contributions, Watkins brought over his wife and children in 1854 to live in Birmingham for six years. By 1861, he was bragging in a newspaper that he had raised money to purchase not only himself but also two sisters and a brother. He ambitiously told an audience that he wanted to bring over his mother to Britain "where he hoped to live and die."

Watkins's trail gets murky after 1860. Perhaps war clouds pulled him back to the United States, where he appeared in the 1860 census for Hartford. Nonetheless, in 1861, the year the Civil War began, he was back in Britain. Watkins, "lecturer on slavery," appeared in the British census in a Manchester boardinghouse. Newspapers featured his lectures, and he continued to lecture until at least 1867.

Then, Watkins disappeared. If he returned to Hartford, he did not appear with his wife, "Mrs. Mary Watkins," in the 1860s city directories or the 1870 census or with the Thomas Watkins who may have been his brother or uncle. Perhaps James Watkins did not return to settle in Hartford or died early, heartbroken because his son Simeon in Hartford died in 1870 from lung problems.

James Watkins's legacy is his slave narrative and any impact he made with his lectures. In addition to providing entertainment, the lectures educated and changed attitudes. Newspapers suggested the impact of Watkins's lectures by reporting on the collection of money and the resolutions and pledges against slavery made after his lectures.

Historian J.M. Blackett points out that Black lecturers' stories of triumph over slavery quickened hopes for the British working class's own struggle. It is clear that Watkins and other abolitionist lecturers educated textile workers, whose livelihoods depended on American cotton. Manchester workers wrote an "entreaty" to Lincoln in support of steps toward abolition of "that foul blot upon civilization and Christianity—chattel slavery." Their letter merited a reply from Lincoln praising their "sublime Christian heroism" and a shipload of relief supplies for those suffering from the closure of many cotton mills.

Chapter 4

RETALIATION FOR ACHIEVING FREEDOM

Matilda and Richard Neal (Anne Arundel),
1849 and 1853

Preserved in the Morris Family Archives is Matilda and Richard Neal's love story. During both slavery and freedom, Matilda and Richard always wanted to be together. They married while enslaved in Anne Arundel County. When manumitted, Richard did not look for another wife. Instead, he tried to buy the freedom of Matilda and their children. When Matilda became impatient and was caught running away with the children, capture did not deter the couple. Richard continued to pursue their audacious wish to live together in freedom and achieved that end by raising sufficient money. When Matilda's owner tried to take his revenge, they triumphed.

Sarah Glen Bland bought Matilda from James Smith and allowed her to live with Bland's daughter Sarah. Isaac Mayo gained control of Matilda through his marriage to Sarah Bland in 1833. He was a career officer in the U.S. Navy who would rise to become commander of the USS *Constitution*, the flagship of the African Squadron.

Matilda's runaway advertisement described her as a "bright [light-skinned] Mulatto," about thirty years old, of "middling size," who wore "her hair twisted up behind as a white person." Matilda's daring hairstyle is a clue to her attractions and her personality. While enslaved, she lived in Anne Arundel County at Gresham, one of Mayo's two properties.

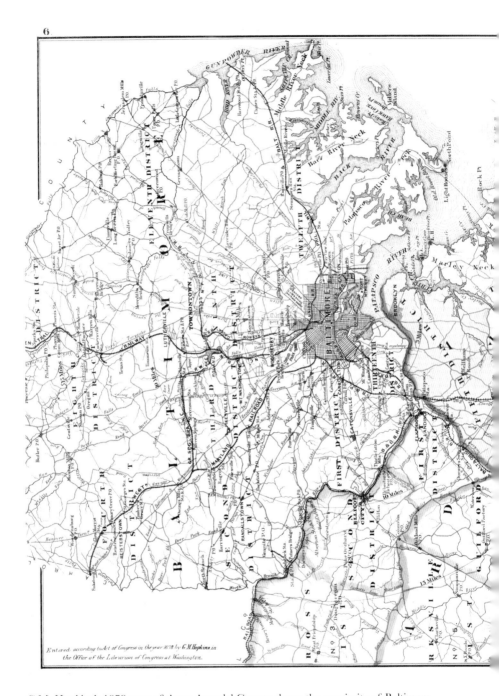

G.M. Hopkins's 1878 map of Anne Arundel County shows the proximity of Baltimore, both for those selling produce and those fleeing from slavery. *Library of Congress.*

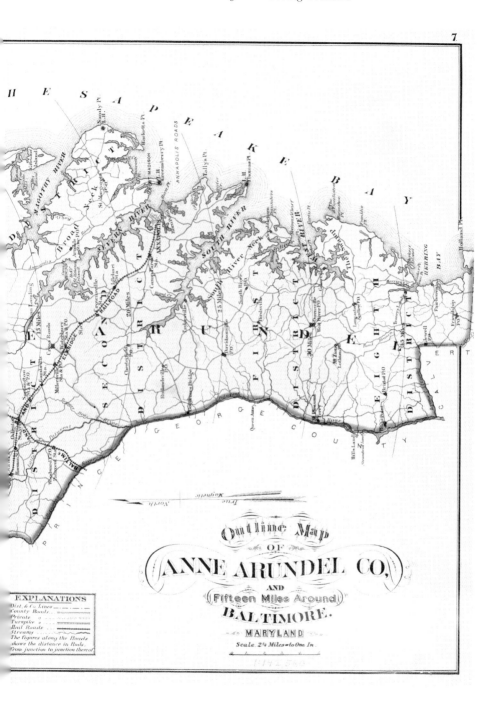

Gresham was situated near Annapolis on Mayo's Neck, a point between the South and Rhode Rivers.

Matilda worked as a "house girl" (housemaid). Among their twenty-three bondsmen, the Mayos favored Matilda. Her resulting "good" treatment meant she only received whippings when Mayo's wife was irritated.

In her twenties, Matilda married Richard "Dicky" Neal(e). Richard was born about 1810 and lived at Ivy Neck, a neighboring farm of 690 acres owned by James Cheston. Cheston also owned Richard's mother and knew his father, who was owned by Virgil Maxey. Cheston was a well-known Baltimore merchant and a contradiction—a slaveholding

Commodore Isaac Mayo had a distinguished career in the U.S. Navy until the Civil War. *Collection of the Maryland State Archives.*

Quaker who would leave behind seventy-seven bondsmen at his death.

Once married, Richard and Matilda did not live together, as they had separate owners and responsibilities. Mayo allotted Matilda separate quarters at Gresham for her and her children. She could thus entertain her husband, who brought her luxuries, meat or clothing to supplement her ration from Mayo. While enslaved, Matilda bore six children and, when free, another four. This meant that in the first years of their marriage, Richard and Matilda had to watch their older children grow up in slavery.

Then, their situation changed radically. Before his death in 1843, Richard's owner, James Cheston, reversed his feelings about slavery. He made his heirs promise to free the people Cheston owned. When the seventy-seven enslaved African Americans were divided among his heirs, his daughter Anne Cheston Morris, to whom Richard was apportioned, remained faithful to James Cheston's wishes. In 1844, Richard Neal, assessed at $400, became a free man at age thirty-three. Using the description in his manumission papers, picture him at

> *about…thirty three…years,…about…5…feet 8 and a half…inches high,…brown…complexion, has…a…scar on his forehead…and… another…on…the…right…cheek…and was raised in the County aforesaid* [Anne Arundel].

For Richard, manumission was a mixed blessing, legally separating him from Matilda and their children. Once free, Richard repeatedly tried to redeem their freedom. Although freed people often sought safety in free states, Richard stayed in Maryland to be near Matilda. Like most other freed Cheston bondsmen, Richard chose to remain at Ivy Neck, where he worked for Anne Morris for about a year.

Because Isaac Mayo believed freedom was "contagious," he consistently blamed the freed "Cheston people" for helping their friends and relatives to run away. In order to dissuade Matilda from escaping, Mayo "gave" a 120-acre island farm to Richard. For the farm, Richard paid the sum of $125 in rent per year. Although the farm was described by a Philadelphia newspaper as "highly improved," the buildings were in bad condition, and Richard had to provide his own farm equipment and livestock. Part of the year, he worked clearing land for a neighbor, Richard Carman. From catching and selling oysters in off hours, Richard earned the cash to pay wages to farm workers. That enabled him to earn a living selling the produce that they raised.

After three years, Richard became frustrated. In 1848, he gave up the unprofitable farm and went to live with his wife at Gresham for about a year. After Richard abandoned the farm, Matilda suffered increasingly under the sway of Mayo and his wife. Richard counseled patience, while he saved money. Matilda, however, tired of her treatment. When Mayo threatened that he would sell Matilda, she believed him, because he had just sold a mother and daughter. Matilda courageously made the decision to seek freedom for herself and her children.

Meanwhile, distrustful of Richard's bad influence, Mayo had moved Matilda and her family to Howard County, forty miles from Anne Arundel County. There, his family owned Blandair, a 620-acre farm in Elkridge. That strategy backfired. Baltimore was a tempting destination, given its large free African American population in which to hide. The move only made Baltimore that much closer. Even if Baltimore was less than twenty miles from Blandair, however, Matilda's escape was impressive. She left in a dangerously large group of seven others in addition to her own five children, ranging from ten months to ten years of age (Rachel, Mary, Emeline, James and Kitty). She did not have the help of her sixth child—the oldest son, Billy—because he had returned to Gresham with Mayo.

At Gresham, Mayo's manager realized that something was amiss when he discovered that Billy had not done his job. The manager was ready to whip Billy for not cleaning or feeding the horse he had driven between Blandair and Gresham. Then, the manager discovered that Billy had disappeared, as

Blandair slave quarters still existed in 1933. *Historic American Buildings Survey, Library of Congress.*

had his family at Blandair. Billy had fled separately from his mother, going by water to Baltimore with Richard's relative John Davis. Like Richard, Davis was a freedman accused of tempting his wife and children to escape.

Mayo's only recourse was to place a runaway advertisement with a $300 reward in October 1849. In the advertisement, Mayo held Richard responsible for the escape. Mayo described Richard, "a dark mulatto and a free man," and the means of escape, "possibly a one-horse carriage." Matilda's fellow bondsman William Hunter would later swear that he, first, had seen Richard persuade the family to pack their clothing and leave and, second, had seen Richard take Matilda and the children from the farm at four o'clock in the morning.

Affidavits, given under oath to Philadelphia's mayor, let Richard and Matilda speak for themselves. Matilda had been convinced all along that Mayo was suspicious of Richard. In her affidavit of February 5, 1853, Matilda was emphatic that Richard was neither present nor encouraging her to flee. Richard was equally adamant that he was not involved. Their version of events does not make Richard's intervention feasible, although their testimony may reflect fear or a desire to protect each other.

Matilda fled in the fall of 1849 but was captured after three or four days. Before her arrest, Matilda claimed to have had no communication with Richard. Indeed, she had no word from him even once she was placed in the

Baltimore jail for two weeks. It was while Matilda was in jail that her fate was sealed. As a result of his anger over the escape, Mayo sold Matilda and her children to the infamous Hope Slatter. Slatter, in turn, sold them to a fellow slave trader from Tennessee named Gordon.

Mayo blamed Richard for his expenses: $700 for the runaway advertisement and a fee for a police officer. But it was Matilda who took the brunt of Mayo's anger. She testified that Mayo threatened to have the slave trader "take us out of the State as far as 'Wind and water would carry us'" and to separate the family "three thousand miles apart." The ultimate blow to Matilda was hearing that the baby was to be sold "away from my breast."

Richard happened to be in Baltimore selling chickens and apples when he heard of a captured freedom seeker resembling Matilda. To discover more, Richard had to find someone to read to him the newspaper with the runaway advertisement. Upon hearing Matilda's description, Richard realized both that he would need a large sum to rescue the family and that he would be blamed. He was forced to turn to someone outside the African American community.

In November 1849, Richard resorted to Dr. Caspar Morris, the husband of Anne Cheston Morris, who had freed Richard. Richard left Baltimore to go to Philadelphia to announce the alarming news of the escape and capture to Dr. Morris. When Richard swore that he was not involved, Dr. Morris believed him and turned to a network of antislavery Quakers for help. Dr. Morris found Richard a job in Philadelphia with Townsend Sharpless, a Quaker dry goods dealer. Then, Richard Neal, Dr. Morris and Townsend Sharpless began the battle with Mayo.

Richard handed over his savings of $500 to Dr. Caspar Morris. He proposed to sell himself and his family back into temporary bondage if Dr. Morris would purchase the family's freedom from the slave trader.

THREE HUNDRED DOLLARS REWARD.— Ran away from the residence of the subscriber, on Elkridge, one bright Mulatto Negro Woman, named MATILDA, about thirty years of age. She always wears her hair twisted up behind as a white person, and is about a middling size. She carried with her five Children, the eldest of which is a Girl, named RACHEL, about ten years of age; the second, a Girl named MARY, is about eight years of age; the third, a Girl named EMELINE, about six years of age; the fourth, a Boy named JAMES, about three years of age; the fifth, a Baby named KITTY, about ten months old.

When she left, she went in company with her husband, Richard Neil, a dark mulatto and a free man, who is suspected to have assisted her and her five children in making their escape in a one horse carriage.

Whoever apprehends said negroes, and secures them so that I get them again, I will pay to him three hundred dollars. ISAAC MAYO. o19-'3t*

Isaac Mayo placed Matilda's runaway advertisement in the *Baltimore Sun. Collection of the Maryland State Archives.*

Caspar Morris was the son-in-law of the former owner of Richard Neal. *Courtesy of the Free Library of Philadelphia, Print and Picture Department.*

The Neal family would work off their debt to Dr. Morris and regain their legal freedom.

Dr. Morris had to tell Richard that he was not financially able to accept the deal. However, by talking to friends, he raised enough to buy Matilda and the baby. Then, because the Neal children were to be separated from one another when sold out of state, Dr. Morris appealed to a wider set of sympathizers in Philadelphia, New York and Boston.

A January 25, 1853 letter Sharpless later wrote to Pennsylvania governor William Bigler included Dr. Morris's appeal to "some of my friends." On the list of donations were $500 from Richard and $300 from his "fellow servants" (perhaps at Ivy Neck). The successful "subscription" came to a total of $3,235.63.

Francis King, a prominent Baltimore Quaker, agreed to act as agent in the purchase of the family. He redeemed the freedom of Matilda and the baby when he caught up to them. He found the trader Gordon at a train stop just after the group had crossed into Virginia. Having left Maryland, the trader was willing to break his agreement with Mayo to separate family members. King promptly sent Matilda and the baby back to Philadelphia, where Dr. Morris's wife made immediate arrangements to manumit them.

King kept following the trail of the rest of the family. Probably buying them in stages as donors sent money, King again intercepted the slave trader in Richmond, where he bought the freedom of another child. A member of the Pulliam slave-trading family bought the remaining children and headed south. King purchased them in Mobile. The children returned by steamer via Savannah to Philadelphia.

The Neal family finally realized their dream to live in freedom. The parents and six children appeared in Philadelphia's Locust Ward in the 1850 census. Richard and Matilda spent the next years working hard. By 1853, Richard had been serving steadily as coachman for Townsend Sharpless since November 1849. Matilda also worked, probably as a laundress or domestic servant, as censuses later documented her doing. The Neals earned their friends' praises. Honesty, industry and virtue were the key words. In 1853, *The Liberator*, an abolitionist newspaper, would sympathetically mention Richard "as an honest, hard-working man." That same year, Dr. Caspar Morris would, in turn, write that since 1849, "they have been living virtuously and have been industrious thriving people."

The story of a wife's escape, her redemption by a freed husband and their reunion in freedom is heartwarming. It is, however, not unique. What is exceptional is the cruel twist of the sequel.

Despite the passage of over three years, Isaac Mayo did not forgive the Neals. Richard's prior attempts to buy Matilda and the children, their courageous escape and their redemption from slavery were affronts to Matilda's former owner. He realized that he could not punish Matilda, but Richard Neal was vulnerable. Somehow, Mayo became informed of the Neals' whereabouts. Isaac Mayo retaliated by arranging to abduct Richard.

Mayo wanted Richard to suffer the brunt of the law in a slave state. He used the excuse of Richard's enticement of various enslaved individuals from Anne Arundel County after his move to Philadelphia. Mayo had political clout with Maryland's governor, E. Louis Lowe. Based on his own sworn testimony and on the word of his bondsman William Hunter, Mayo persuaded Governor Lowe to act. Governor Lowe issued a requisition to Pennsylvania's governor, William Bigler for the arrest and extradition of Richard. Governor Lowe, however, made a crucial mistake in the papers by accusing Richard of being a "fugitive slave" rather than a "fugitive from justice."

Mayo put his dramatic plan to abduct Richard into execution in 1853. He appointed Officer John Lamb from Annapolis as his agent. With Governor Bigler's warrant, Lamb attempted to whisk Richard back to Maryland as a criminal. Officer Lamb and two Philadelphia officers arrested Richard on January 25, 1853, at the stable where he worked. Mayo told Richard that he was needed as a witness against John Davis, charged with helping Billy run away. With Richard in custody, Lamb and the Philadelphia officers went to the courthouse to fruitlessly search for a judge. Instead, they ended up at the office of an alderman named Kenney. Kenney quickly heard the men identify Richard as the culprit and approved Lamb's arrest. Rushed along by

William Bigler was governor of Pennsylvania from 1852 to 1855 and represented the state in the United States Senate between 1856 and 1861. *Library of Congress.*

Mayo, the officers dragged Richard into a carriage. Richard had no chance to protest or to inform his family, friends or employer.

While Lamb and the other officers went directly to the Philadelphia, Wilmington and Baltimore Train Station, Mayo stopped at the Neals' residence to gloat. He directed himself to the children because Matilda was at work. Billy's affidavit quoted Mayo. Telling them that their father was in his clutches and already on his way to Maryland, Mayo threatened the children that "they would never see him [Richard] again."

By the time Lamb and his prisoner reached the Philadelphia train station, the afternoon train had already left. Leaving Mayo behind in his hurry, Lamb chose to continue in the carriage to Chester, Pennsylvania, to catch the night mail train continuing southward. However, Lamb made a serious mistake by not crossing into the slave state of Delaware, where the certificate of removal would be effective.

Along the way, the carriage had to stop near Darby in order for the horses to get water. Taking advantage of the stop, Richard jumped out of a carriage window. He led a chase for two miles across the snowy countryside, until a fleet-footed officer caught him and hit him on the head. With Richard, the carriage continued on to Chester. In Chester, Mayo's party had supper at Goff's Hotel while waiting to take the train. An alert Black hotel waiter managed to spread word to the town that a man was on his way back to slavery. A crowd of White abolitionists and sympathetic African Americans assembled.

Meanwhile, the other Neals mobilized help in Philadelphia. The children, who had been frightened by Mayo's bragging, raised the alarm to their mother, their father's employer and the Neals' protector, Dr. Caspar Morris. Mayo and his henchman John Lamb became pitted against the friends of the Neals and the Pennsylvania Abolition Society.

After picking up Richard's freedom papers to prove his status, Dr. Morris and Townsend Sharpless sought out legal help. They turned to former mayor Peter McCall, Francis Wharton and Pemberton Morris, a cousin of Dr. Morris. The lawyers sympathized with Richard, who was overwhelmed by the unexpected and unwarranted seizure. The allies procured a writ of habeas corpus from a county judge in Philadelphia calling for the presentation of Richard before the court.

Dr. Morris and his son followed Richard's trail to the station house. Discovering that, indeed, there had been an arrest, they continued to the railroad station from which the captors' carriage had left. Accompanied by members of the Abolition Society and a police officer, the sons of Morris and Sharpless followed the carriage. They needed to deliver the writ of habeas corpus to Lamb before he could take Richard into Maryland. When the night train south reached Chester, it was a gratifying surprise to find Mayo's officers trying to force Richard onto that very train. Mayo, also on the train, was urgently hurrying the officers.

Even without the Philadelphia contingent, Richard had allies. Public opinion in Chester was sensitive to the kidnapping issue because of Joseph Miller's recent murder while trying to rescue a free teenager from slave catchers. At the Chester station, what *The Liberator* called "friends of the prisoner and a crowd of blacks" had gathered. Richard's captors feared an attempted rescue. As Lamb tried to push Richard onto the train south, members of the crowd pulled. The conductor tired of waiting for a resolution and signaled the engineer to leave.

Because Lamb and his charge did not board the train, the abolitionists could confront them. When the Philadelphians presented the writ, however, their opponents rejected it on the technicalities that the warrant from the governor trumped the writ and that the writ was invalid in the local jurisdiction. Waving his pistol, Mayo threatened one bearer of the writ who had taken hold of Richard. According to an anonymous letter in the *New York Evangelist*, the youth proclaimed, "You are now in a free State, fire if you dare." Mayo backed off.

Due to a snowstorm and the crowd, Mayo and his henchmen decided to spend the night in Chester. Mayo's group prudently lodged Richard in the Chester jail. Richard was reassured by the presence of a crowd of Blacks surrounding the jail. The crowd made it impossible for Mayo to try to sneak Richard into Delaware. Worried, Mayo and a bottle of brandy kept watch inside the jail. Meanwhile, Richard was handcuffed and chained to the floor. Thus passed the night of January 25.

After the fiasco, the abolitionists returned to Philadelphia for a new writ. To start the process, they had to rouse first lawyer Peter McCall and then the chief clerk of the court. The next stop was the supreme court justices' hotel. With the writ in hand, the abolitionists returned to Chester on the earliest train.

That same morning of January 26, Mayo and the officers took Richard to the train south. They were followed by Chester African Americans enlisted by two local Black leaders, Sammy Smith and Edward M. Farris. By the time Richard reached the train platform, "several hundred citizens…were awaiting the course of events," according to the *Chester County Republican*.

The abolitionists had returned triumphantly. With them was the officer of the court bearing the writ of habeas corpus from the Supreme Court. The writ necessitated the appearance of Richard and Mayo in

Philadelphia, notwithstanding Governor Bigler's warrant carrying the seal of Pennsylvania. One of the Philadelphia police officers executing the writ unlocked Richard's handcuffs, and a young abolitionist bought Richard breakfast. An odd party then traveled together to Philadelphia by carriage. The abolitionists and Neal were comfortably inside, but Mayo willingly rode on top in the cold so he could escape the aroused citizens of Chester. Mayo's associates had to take the train back.

After procuring the writ, the abolitionists had taken the precaution of sending one of Dr. Morris's sons to the governor in Harrisburg. The son carried letters begging a stay of execution against the governor's warrant of arrest on the grounds that Richard was not living in Maryland at the time of the alleged enticement. The governor agreed but deferred action and cannily sent his secretary to monitor the trial.

On January 27, 1853, the question before the Pennsylvania Supreme Court was whether Richard was a fugitive of justice accused of enticement. On January 26, the district attorney telegraphed Governor Bigler for copies of the requisition and affidavit from Maryland's governor. As a reply had not yet come and the courtroom was so packed that the air was unpleasant, there was a postponement.

McCall, Wharton and Pemberton Morris constituted Richard's legal counsel. Richard was duly presented before the supreme court, but neither John Lamb nor Mayo appeared in court on Friday, January 28. John Lamb's excuse was not having recovered from a beating during the melee at the train station. That excuse gave Lamb time to leave the state and avoid possible legal retribution. Mayo asserted a convenient need to report to his squadron at Norfolk and also left Pennsylvania.

A delay was granted until Monday, February 1, for passage of the three days allowed by law for return of a fugitive to the proper jurisdiction. By then, the governors had sent telegrams back and forth. All waited anxiously for the resolution of what even the conservative *Evening Bulletin* called a "kidnapping under a legal process."

Mayo conceded by again not appearing in court. Lacking either Mayo or Lamb to give testimony on Richard's rightful return to Maryland, Chief Justice Jeremiah S. Black and his associates, Judges Ellis Lewis, Walter H. Lowrie and George W. Woodward, discussed the matter. They decided to discharge Richard, who was jailed when not in court. Governor Bigler's intervention was not needed, after all.

Ironically, Mayo was reporting to the African Squadron, which prevented the smuggling of Africans into the United States to enslave them.

At one point, the USS *Constitution* served as the flagship of the African Squadron. *NH 63532, Courtesy of the Naval History and Heritage Command.*

Interestingly, Mayo's biographer does not mention the abduction and the trial, only quoting a letter from Mayo, which said:

> *There is another source from which I have been and shall always expect to be annoyed. The Abolitionists—they denounced me as unfit for the Navy because I recaptured seven out of some fifteen or more of my* [enslaved] *servants which had been enticed from me.*

Commenting on the case, the Philadelphia *Sunday Dispatch* underscored the importance of guarding the liberty of every citizen, regardless of color. West Chester's *Jeffersonian* described Richard's own response: "Richard, surrounded by rejoicing friends of both colors left the room in high spirits."

The Neals were once again together. Knowledge of their subsequent lives must be gleaned from the United States Censuses and the research of a Morris descendant. In 1850, Richard was listed as farmer, and the couple had six children, age eleven and under. In 1860, Richard was a coachman, living with Matilda, a washerwoman, and six children, of whom the eldest was a servant. By June 1870, the household included Richard and Matilda, two adult children and four younger ones; the household was supported by Richard's work as a coachman, Matilda's as a domestic employee and Mary's as a dressmaker. It is not clear whether by 1880 Richard had become a waiter, as reported by the census. According to the 1881 city directory, he was still a coachman. At any rate, in 1880, Richard, now widowed, lived with four schoolteaching children in their twenties and thirties and two teenagers in school. The education of the children points to their parents' aspirations for them.

The Neals did not forget Maryland. Three sons (Daniel A., Richard and William) moved back to Anne Arundel County. That is where Richard and his daughter died in 1881 at what the *Christian Recorder* called Richard's "summer home," West River.

Chapter 5

A NETWORK OF AFRICAN AMERICAN UNDERGROUND RAILROAD AGENTS

ISAAC MASON (KENT), 1846

In 1893, Isaac Mason became the author of *The Life of Isaac Mason as a Slave*. He was seventy-one years old. Mason did not attempt his autobiography sooner, he said, because he "lacked educational advantages." He had grown up enslaved in Maryland, where slave owners prohibited him an education. It took a small girl in Worcester to teach him his letters when he was an adult.

Mason was, however, eminently qualified to write the slave narrative *The Life of Isaac Mason as a Slave*. He was articulate about his past. Having fled slavery, he was well familiar with the institution and the desire for freedom. In 1897, the *Worcester Telegram* declared that "his recollections…[were] minute and accurate."

Mason was not ashamed of his background in slavery. He spoke out publicly against slavery, as well as for racial advancement. The *Worcester Telegram* remembered, "He was a prominent figure in the abolitionist demonstrations in Worcester in antebellum days." Mason served as president of the Worcester County Anti-Slavery and Temperance Society of Colored Citizens and on the executive committee of the Worcester County South Division Anti-Slavery Society.

Like his Worcester contemporaries Bethany Veney and Allen Parker, who published slave narratives in 1893 and 1895, respectively, Mason felt he should write a book. *The Life of Isaac Mason as a Slave* came out at a time when aging leaders of the African American community felt all Worcesterites, especially

James Mansfield's residence now houses the Kent Cultural Alliance and features a modern portrait of Isaac Mason. *John Schratwieser, Kent Cultural Alliance.*

the African Americans, needed to remember the ugly, brutal institution of slavery and the courage and initiative of those who escaped it.

The 1890s were a dark time, so younger Black leaders were more radical. Blacks were particularly stricken by the depression. They felt economically and politically marginalized by competition with White immigrants. Blacks had always voted for the Republicans, but Mason attended local meetings of disgruntled Republicans who wanted jobs and attention in return for their loyalty. Blacks felt betrayed by a party and a society that permitted lynchings, the Ku Klux Klan and Jim Crow.

The authors of the narratives wanted to imprint their generation's suffering as well as its initiative, resourcefulness and courage on the collective memory of the African American community. Now that the community's abolitionist allies had died or switched focus, narratives of slavery were meant to reinvigorate the community's own struggle for equality and fair treatment. As historian Janette Thomas Greenwood noted, older African American leaders agreed with statesman Frederick Douglass "'that black memory was a weapon' against injustice."

For these reasons, *The Life of Isaac Mason as a Slave* focused on "that ever memorable period of my life," Mason's years in slavery and his escape. To engage as well as instruct, Mason wrote his autobiography as a horror story,

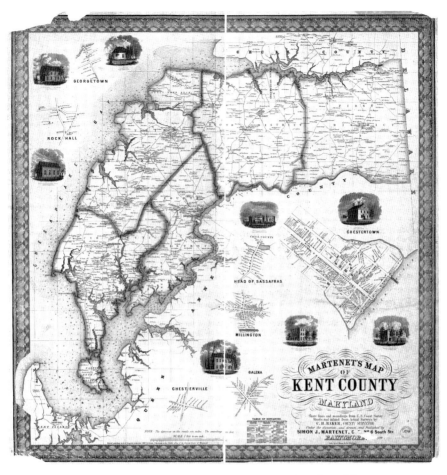

Martenet's 1860 map of Kent County shows Chestertown, where Isaac Mason was enslaved. *Library of Congress.*

an adventure and a religious parable. Despite his suffering, Mason meant to convey how his life had been shaped by faith in God, by assertion of his manhood through resistance and by help from courageous allies.

The owners of Isaac Mason called him Will Thompson, so during his enslavement and escape, the protagonist will be called by his slave name. Will came from Kent County on the Eastern Shore of the Chesapeake Bay. Unlike many in bondage, Will could identify May 14, 1822, as his date of birth in Georgetown "Cross Oats [Cross Roads]" (now Galena). He was the first of four sons and a daughter of Zekiel (Ezekiel) and Sophia Grimes Thompson. Hannah Perkins Woodland, the widow of sea captain Isaac Woodland, owned Will's mother. Although his father was free, Will commented bitterly, "still he had no claim to me." Will, like his brothers and sister, inherited his mother's enslaved condition and added to his owner's capital.

Hannah Woodland placed Will's maternal grandfather, Richard Graham Grimes, in charge of one of her two farms, because, as Will said, she "considered [him] faithful and trustworthy." She made Will's father an overseer and Will's mother a house servant. Perhaps because of his relatives' status, when Will began work at age five, Woodland had him wait on her and run errands. If he avoided more demanding and demeaning field work, instead he had to be available both day and night. Will even slept in a trundle bed in his owner's bedroom.

Change came when Hannah Woodland died at age ninety, when Will was fifteen. Woodland's executor was her son-in-law Hugh Wallis (Wallace), husband of Margaret, one of Woodland's four daughters. Wallis was a prominent slaveholder whose 1857 estate inventory would list land worth $12,370 and nine bondsmen.

The settlement of Woodland's estate upset the status quo. Isaac Taylor bought the farm where the Thompsons lived but not the bondsmen. Through an unpaid debt, Wallis became owner of eight of Woodland's bondsmen. The will freed Sophia's father, Richard Graham Grimes. With a guarantor, Zekiel Thompson was able to buy his ailing wife, Sophia, and his small daughter, Ellen, for $600. Wallis's brother-in-law James Mansfield Jr. purchased the "boy Bill 13" for $250.

Will began the new regime by paying off his dead owner's twenty-five-dollar debt to "Dr. Hyde" (James Heighe) through hard work around Hyde's house and barn. Faced with daily whippings and withholding of food, Will did not remain compliant. His stay at Dr. Hyde's ended on a day when Hyde's wife beat Will and he shoved her to the ground. Will escaped punishment by jumping out the window and running to hide in the hay in the barn. The next day, he fled first to his mother and then to his grandfather before they unhappily sent him back to the farm of Hugh Wallis.

Will's bad behavior had ramifications. Hyde withdrew his surety for the payment to purchase Ellen and Sophia and demanded that Zekiel pay him the impossible sum. Ellen and Sophia avoided return to slavery by flight to Baltimore, where they chanced upon a Quaker willing to pay the debt. Mother and daughter became free but at the cost of family separation. Until she was sixteen, Ellen remained working in the Quaker's household. Happily, then, the Quaker summoned Sophia and Zekiel to make the manumission of Sophia and Ellen official.

Isaac Mason's image appeared on the frontispiece of his 1893 book. *Documenting the American South, University of North Carolina at Chapel Hill Library.*

Isaac Mason.

James Mansfield Jr., Will's owner, now took over Will's supervision. Mansfield was a cabinetmaker, coffin maker and undertaker. Initially, Will worked for Mansfield's wife in the house in Chestertown, Kent's county seat. Mrs. Mansfield took a dislike to Will and told her husband to give him a brutal beating daily. When Mansfield became disgusted at beating Will to please his wife, he transferred Will to his sixty-acre farm.

Will worked hard to increase Mansfield's yield of corn. He also helped in Mansfield's undertaking business by driving the hearse. His performance pleased Mansfield. Just before Christmas, Mansfield gave Will a new suit and a chance to accompany him aboard the sloop *George Washington* to sell corn and wheat in Baltimore. Unfortunately, the trip became traumatic when Will angered two White men and received a beating to teach him urban etiquette for enslaved African Americans.

In August 1846, Will made another serious mistake, offending both Mansfield and Wallis. Will disobeyed a visiting Wallis daughter (Mansfield's niece) by throwing spoiled meat to the dogs rather than eating it. When

James Mansfield heard what had happened, he ordered Will to the cellar for punishment. Not understanding why, Will reacted: "Though a slave and his property, yet I dared to assert the lion of my manhood that he had aroused in me." Mansfield shot at Will three times. Uninjured, Will fled and spent Saturday night in a mulberry thicket. On Sunday, he desperately needed spiritual comfort, but Mansfield was the preacher at both the White and Black Methodist churches. Will lamented, "I had no one to speak to but God," but he believed God responded by sending another bondsman to Will with food.

Will had no alternative. He had to return, although the rebellion undermined Mansfield's authority. Mansfield compensated by deviously using Wallis to back him up. Thinking himself forgiven, Will continued working on Mansfield's farm. In November, Mansfield tricked him into running an errand at Wallis's place at Morgan's Creek Neck. Because of the note Will innocently carried to Wallis, Wallis beat Will with a pitchfork. Will fled, outrunning Wallis and his son. On the way back to Mansfield's, he tried to cross a creek. He was swept into deep water but attributed his ability to save himself to God's help.

In December, Will discovered the depth of his owner's deceit. Mansfield sent Will to Wallis's for wood. Will tried to avoid trouble by evading Wallis but still had to struggle with Wallis's bondsmen. Victorious, Will headed to Mansfield's, where he avoided Wallis a second time. Then, while he was unloading the wood someone else had delivered for him, he resolved to lay his trust in God.

Will's faith was justified. That evening, Mansfield's son privately revealed that his father had agreed to sell Will to Wallis. Wallis planned, in turn, to send him for sale in New Orleans in early January. Will decided to determine his own fate beforehand by escaping with Josh, another Mansfield bondsman whom Will trusted.

Using oats saved from the feed of Mansfield's horse, Will hired a horse from an old African American man named Jim Willmer. In secrecy, Will rode to Georgetown Cross Roads to enlist someone known since Will's childhood. For nine dollars, Joe Brown agreed to guide Will, Josh and a Wallis bondsman named George to Philadelphia over Christmas. Meanwhile, to supplement their scanty savings, Josh and Will earned twelve dollars more by working odd jobs at night.

For Christmas, Will received the customary special meal, days off and gift of fifty cents. Mansfield unsuspectingly gave Will permission to visit his family at Georgetown Cross Roads. Using that opportunity, on Christmas

1846, Will would later remember that he and Josh bid adieu to "cares and lashes, and started for the land of liberty and a city where we could breathe the refreshing air of freedom." On the way, they met George, who had found a boat for them to cross the nearby creek. Then, all set off on their journey.

The freedom seekers arrived at Georgetown Cross Roads only to find Brown drunk. Josh and George were ready to turn back. Will had to be quite persuasive to get them to hide in his mother's attic. Surprisingly, that afternoon, Brown showed up with instructions to meet at Price's Wood in the evening and to use the sign and countersign "Yea! yo!" and "Friend to the guard!" When they met, Brown took charge. The men knelt in the snow to pray and then took the solemn oath "to fight for each other till we died." The freedom seekers paid Brown his fee, "the liberation money," and all prepared themselves with a hearty meal of bread and meat.

The freedom seekers set out by night for Wilmington, Delaware, about thirty-five miles away through slave territory. Approaching Wilmington, Brown was cautious and stopped to consult an old Black acquaintance. There was appalling news. Kidnappers were waiting by the bridge into the city.

The old man advised them to choose another route. Brown went to reconnoiter, while the other three spent an unforgettable day in the woods hiding under a fallen tree. Around them surged fifty White foxhunters and their hounds. Will's companions shivered with fear and begged to turn back. Will had to agree. With forethought, he had learned to navigate by the North Star, which his teacher had said "the Lord had placed…to lead people out of slavery." Once the star became visible, Will remembered his teacher's words and led them north, despite their resolution to turn back.

After five miles, lo and behold, Will, Josh and George met Brown and their second guide—Perry Augustus. They followed Augustus past Wilmington to Pennsylvania, their guide having proven trustworthy. As Will would recall, the freedom seekers crossed the state border "from bondage into liberty, from darkness into light." They felt "joy and gratitude." At Will's suggestion, Augustus and the rest knelt to gratefully thank God.

Proceeding ten miles further into Chester County, the freedom seekers arrived at what Will called a "little heaven on earth for a fugitive." They had reached New Garden, a Quaker community and a stop on the Underground Railroad. Nelson Wiggins, a member of the local African Methodist Episcopal Church, opened his home, providing them with breakfast and beds. For two days, the travelers relaxed. They were congratulated by many on their newfound liberty, including by those Will called his "companions in slavery once, now companions in freedom."

$200 Reward.

Ranaway from the subscriber on Saturday night last, two negro men named Bill Thompson and Josh Woodland.

Bill is about 5 feet 9 or 10 inches high, dark complected, swaggers very much when he walks. had on when he left a casinet coat and pantaloons and a glazed cap.

Josh is about 5 feet 6 or 7 inches high, a mulatto, the fore finger of one of his hands is off at the first joint, had on when he left a casinet roundabout and pantaloons. They both taken other clothing with them.

I will give the above reward to any person or persons who will arrest them and put them in prison, so that I can get them again.

JAMES MANSFIELD.
Chester Town, Md. jan'y 1, '47.

Mason wrote that his slave name was Will, but he was called Bill in the runaway advertisement and on the estate inventory. *Collection of Maryland State Archives.*

Will, Josh and George left the oasis of the Wiggins home. Unable to find local work, they continued to Philadelphia. They reached and wondered at Philadelphia. Then, they wandered. Tired and suffering from swollen feet, the freedom seekers chanced upon an old Black "gentleman" one Sunday, who cared for them. The next Sunday, he took them to his church, where a woman had news of work. Will quickly took advantage of the offer and stayed in Chester County. Only two weeks had passed since they had left Georgetown Cross Roads.

Will wrote that he became a farm hand for James Pile for "four dollars a month, board, lodging, and washing." He was happy to choose for himself and be paid. After three years of threshing wheat, quarrying and cutting wood, Will felt safe. When another farmer, Joshua Pusey, offered work for "50 cents a day, a house to live and two acres of planting land for my own use," he was elated. He imagined himself comfortably married to his fiancée, Anna.

This dream evaporated in August 1849. A notorious slave catcher, Thomas McCreary, barged into freedom seeker Tom Mitchell's home at midnight. McCreary dragged Mitchell, half-dressed, to the train in order to take him to a Baltimore slave pen. Presumably, he would sell Mitchell in New Orleans. Will was unnerved. Mitchell was a fellow freedom seeker from the Eastern Shore and lived nearby. Even though Chester County Quakers managed to buy Mitchell's freedom and bring him back, Will was still scared. He fled to Philadelphia, where he found a job as a hod carrier. He only returned to Chester County in September 1849, long enough to marry Anna and bring her back to Philadelphia.

Will may or may not have known that Mansfield was actively seeking him and Josh. On January 2, 1847, the *Kent News* had published a runaway advertisement placed by James Mansfield for the capture of "two negro men named Bill Thompson and Josh Woodland." Mansfield described "Bill" as:

> about 5 feet 9 or 10 inches high, dark complected, swaggers very much when he walks. Had on when he left a casinet [mix of cotton and wool] coat and pantaloons and a glazed cap.

Henry H. Brown was a Black leader in Worcester with Underground Railroad contacts. *American Antiquarian Society.*

In 1850, the passage of the Fugitive Slave Act emboldened slave owners. While at work, Will caught sight of Hugh Wallis's son. Abolitionist lawyer David Paul Brown helped African American leaders in Philadelphia to confirm Wallis was there in pursuit of freedom seekers. The leaders advised Will and Anna to head north quickly and gave them an introductory letter to Jacob Gibbs of the New York City Underground Railroad.

The couple sold their belongings and fled. At the dock in New York, a hack driver tried to waylay the couple while they awaited Gibbs. Gibbs rescued them, in the process receiving a beating. Once recovered, Gibbs took them to the steamboat bound for Fall River, Massachusetts. After he left them, they discovered that he had cheated them on the tickets by buying second- instead of first-class tickets. This so embarrassed Will in front of his new wife that he spent scarce money to buy her a seat in first class.

From Fall River, the couple caught a train to Boston, only to find that their contact there had died. Somehow, they connected with Lewis Hayden, a freedom seeker active in helping others like himself. The Boston Vigilance Committee paid board for Anna and Will so they could stay with the Haydens for several weeks. By now, Will was using the name Isaac Mason, according to the committee treasurer's records, so from now on he will be called Isaac Mason here.

```
Nov. 13 Friend by Rev John Parkman                    5
  "   16 Two Friends at  Salem (A.M.&L H C)
            by E G Loring                            20
          Amount carried over                      341 35


[p. 5] The Vigilance  Committee          Dr.


  1850
  Nov.      Amount br'ot forward                    44 21
   "        Peter Kelly for posting 300 bills)
   "          describing the personal appear-  }     3
   "          ance of Slave Hunters           )
   "    16  Isabella S Holmes (Father Snow-
              dons daughter) for boarding James
              Dale wife & child 2 weeks Fugitive)
              do Henry Garnet 2 W & 5 days    "  )
              do George Johnson      do       "  )
              do David Brown         do       "  }19 25
              do Henry Richardson 1 do        "  )
              do Ely Baney         1 do 5"    "  )
              do Catherine Jones   1 do 5"    "  )
              do Henry Williams       3       "  )
              do Henry Lewis in all to 28.75     )
              deduct am. paid by Lewis       )
              Hayden  9.50                  )
   "    "   John R Taylor boarding Henry
              Long & Jones                 "        10
   "    "   Susan Burroughs do Joseph Truet
              Wife & 2 ch.                  20 )
              deduct am. paid by L. Hayden7 50)12 50
   "    "   Lewis Hayden boarding Fugitives
              John Simmons  Wm Miller        )
              Ja. Jackson  Solomon Banks     } 43 87
              Geo. Reason   Isaac Mason &    )
              Wife                           )
  Dec. 12   Wright & Hasty Printing 2000      )
   "          Handbills Warning Fugitives &   }     5
              the People against Slave Hunters)
   "    26  Isabella S Holmes boarding Geo.
              Newton  Fugitive                     3 43
1851Jan.2   James J Johnson do Jas. Tompson
              Fugitive                             6
   "     3  Damrell & Moore Printing 1000 Cir-
              culars                              11
            Samuel Flint boarding __Thomas
              Wife & 2 ch.                         5
            Wm C Nell cash  to Fugitives 40.65
              & his Services 42.45              83 10
   "    10  viz Henry Gardner-Wm Crafts & Wife-
              Andrew Jones-Wm Stewart  Edwd. Gray
              Elizth Higgerman-James Cork-Jas.
              Brown-Fugitives
                          Amt. forward           246 36
```

Wilbur Siebert transcribed the Boston Vigilance Committee treasurer's records for his famous Underground Railroad collection. *Ohio History Connection.*

Lewis Hayden's house still stands on Beacon Hill in Boston. *Courtesy of National Parks of Boston.*

Isaac Mason needed a job. Underground Railroad agents conferred back and forth with Martin Stowell, a White abolitionist in Worcester. It was decided that Anna would stay in the care of the Haydens while Isaac went to Worcester. Isaac carried a fateful letter from William C. Nell of the Boston Vigilance Committee to William H. Brown, a leader in Worcester's African American community.

Mason came to Worcester in the fall of 1850. He soon had an inkling that Worcester offered, as he put it, "plenty of good employment and benevolent sympathizers." In the African American community, help came from upholsterer William Brown, and in the White from abolitionist Martin Stowell and politician George Hoar. Mason lodged at Ebenezer Hemenway's boardinghouse and found work.

Mason discovered that Worcester had a supportive abolitionist community, including Stephen and Abby Kelley Foster, Samuel May and Thomas Wentworth Higginson. During the decade in which Mason arrived, the abolitionists showed their mettle. Clark University historian Janette Greenwood called Worcester's mid-decade reputation "far more radical" than Boston's.

The new Fugitive Slave Act sparked a tumultuous protest meeting. Two outraged freedom seekers spontaneously testified to their experience in slavery—one could have been Mason. Throughout the rest of the 1850s, Worcester activists passionately continued to fight slavery by involvement in the attempted rescue of Anthony Burns, Bleeding Kansas and John Brown's Raid. In October 1854, when locals suspected the notorious United States marshal Asa Butman of coming to town to arrest freedom seekers, Butman barely escaped from the city ahead of the crowd chasing him.

In 1855, Worcester would pride itself as "Canada to the Slave," but beforehand, in 1851, locals advised Mason to flee slave hunters again. By now, Anna was living in Worcester with Isaac, so Isaac accompanied Anna to safety in Boston.

In April 1851, Mason and two others at risk fled to Canada by train. Snowy Montreal proved cold both in its weather and its welcome. The men moved on to Toronto. Their first job ended disastrously, and their belongings were seized for debt. The situation worsened when their next employer, in Queen's Bush, cheated them of their wages for cutting wood. Mason went to Toronto to track the employer's employer. With no success, he persuaded an acquaintance to write a letter for him requesting money from Worcester. By working off the debt for his belongings, Mason reclaimed his wedding suit and boots. He used the funds from Worcester for his board. Just then, Mason was shocked to receive a letter announcing his wife's illness. He felt compelled to return to Worcester as soon as possible to be by his wife's side. The illness was likely related to the birth of their eldest child, Eliza Jane, on July 25, 1851. Sadly, Eliza Jane would live less than a year.

The trip back to Worcester took Mason two weeks, which were filled with anxiety, deprivation and exhaustion. Without money, he had to be resourceful. Mason persuaded a steamboat captain to let him work his way across Lake Ontario to Rochester. From there, he had no recourse but to walk. Guided by railroad tracks, he covered an incredible seventy-five miles in one night. Thinking to spare his feet, he switched to the towpath along the Erie Canal. A kind canalboat captain offered to let him sleep by day on his boat, if by night Mason would ride the horse towing the boat.

Mason thought himself set for a safe return. He was mistaken. In Utica, he looked up as the canalboat passed under a bridge. To his horror, he glimpsed his nemesis, Wallis. Even though Wallis did not recognize him, Mason wrote that he became determined to be "as agile as a hare and as cunning as a fox." He switched routes.

Night and day, he walked the main road, becoming exhausted and hungry. At Albany, he sheltered from a storm in a stopped freight car. When he awakened, he was happy to find the train had transported him ten miles closer to Worcester. After leaving the car, he chanced on a camp meeting. After all his trials, the companionship and prayer boosted his spirits. Mason walked on to Worcester, arriving on July 2, 1851.

The Life of Isaac Mason as a Slave might have ended when Mason was united with his wife and baby. Instead, Mason could not refrain from adding a last adventure which he justified as "benefitting my condition or the advancement of the human family." He wanted to investigate a future in Haiti.

Haiti was the hemisphere's African American republic, created by a revolution of the enslaved. Scottish journalist James Redpath was promoting Haiti and setting up a system of recruiters. Haiti's president, Fabre Geffrard, welcomed American Blacks, offering citizenship, land and advances on passage. One proponent of emigration was Henry Highland Garnet, who, like Mason, was born enslaved in Kent County. Garnet saw emigration as an antidote for African American hopelessness about rights and racism and as a means for promoting Black nationalism.

Mason accompanied seventy-five emigrants to Haiti on May 14, 1860, sailing from Boston on the *Pearl* under Captain Porter. Mason discovered that Haiti was hospitable and fertile, as promised, but also hot and disease-ridden. He found the emigrants' settlements poorly situated and equipped and the emigrants' many problems unmentioned and unmitigated by either the Haitian government or Redpath.

Not only did gales at sea and a tropical disease almost cost Mason his life, but Haiti was also a disillusionment. Luckily, Mason was free to return. He had paid his own passage and so was not entangled in the sharecropper-like system. He carried back 325 letters from emigrants. Mason wrote to Worcester papers that Haiti was "only a premature graveyard for the race." He concluded his book by writing that "my return and the expressions contained in the letters broke up Haytian emigration." He overstated his role, since the movement continued into 1862.

After thanking God for His protection while shipboard and in Haiti, *The Life of Isaac Mason as a Slave*'s last words were: "I then made up my mind that Worcester should be my future home, and here I should dwell until the end of my days."

There is documentation that Mason did indeed remain in Worcester until his death. Mason flourished insofar as permitted by Worcester's White society, given discrimination and exclusion of African Americans from the main industry, manufacturing. Mason built a reputation through his persistence and hard work. In 1856, Isaac and Anna reached a milestone—owning property in a city where most residents did not own their homes.

Former landlord Ebenezer Hemenway was a role model for Mason. After working as a farmer, then a day laborer and jobber, Mason received a break in 1857 that enabled him to take city janitorial jobs, as had Hemenway. Washing privies and cleaning was menial but steady work, continuing through the 1860s. Then, starting in 1860, Mason also became a "carpet cleaner" like Hemenway, meaning he cleaned not only carpets but also houses and windows. Mason was proud enough to represent his trade in the 1865 Fourth of July parade. He was successful enough to pay for listings in the city directories in 1889, 1890 and 1892. Up to the end of his life, Mason continued to be listed as a carpet cleaner—for instance, at remarriage in 1894 and at death in 1898.

Mason maintained his tie to Maryland. By 1860, Worcester's small African American community included thirty-five freedom seekers born in Maryland. In 1866, Isaac Mason returned to Maryland to examine the condition of freedmen with Reverend George Offley's African Methodist Episcopal Zion Annual Conference mission. Mason kept up with Maryland relatives. Mason's younger brother, known as William Anderson, migrated to Worcester, and the family knew of another brother, Michael Thompson, who lived in Vicksburg, Mississippi.

Mason became a local leader. During the Civil War, Mason was a military recruiter for the United States Colored Troops. He represented Worcester's African American community in Boston and knew men of national stature, such as Francis Jackson and Lewis Hayden. Mason attended Black conventions and joined in the ongoing equal rights struggle. He stepped forward to help fellow refugees arriving during the Civil War, and Mason's cohort came to ally with these refugees in politics, civil rights advocacy, fraternal orders and establishment of the Bethel AME Church.

As early as the 1870s, Mason lived in a world in which African Americans networked outside Worcester, enjoyed secular and religious social activities and belonged to mutual aid societies through the African Methodist Episcopal Church and fraternal lodges. In this world, women and men with menial jobs, whether born free or enslaved, could show off their talents. Mason served as city- and regionwide officer and committee member in the orders of the Prince Hall Masons, Good Samaritans and Odd Fellows. He attained the status of Right Worthy Grand Chief of the Good Samaritans. In September 1893, at age seventy, he was still marching in the Attleboro parade of the Colored Odd Fellows as a past Grand Master.

Isaac Mason was one of the generation born in slavery who rose to prominence. His activities in Worcester showed the finesse developed by African Americans through participation in "colored conventions" and veterans organizations, as well as fraternal orders and churches. His generation faced and had to shield themselves from White hostility, yet they kept a vision of full future citizenship. Mason's voice was among those calling for what historian Nick Salvatore phrased as "moral uplift and personal rectitude…[and] freedom and equality."

When he turned seventy-five, the *Worcester Telegram*, on May 15, 1897, praised Isaac Mason:

> *A man of unusual native ability and shrewdness, Mr. Mason's success in rising above the circumstances in which he was placed followed him in later life, and he has for years been looked up to by his people…as a counselor and a friend and his voice and judgement have been followed on many occasions.*

At Mason's death, despite the rise of younger, more assertive Black leaders, the *Worcester Telegram*, on August 27, 1898, had the headline, "Born in Slavery, Dies a Leader." It called Mason "one of the most honored men of his race in Worcester." United States senator George Hoar, Mason's fifty-year friend, gave Mason's eulogy at the Bethel African Methodist Episcopal Church that Mason had helped to found. Hoar praised Mason for doing "his best always for his race." Any impact of Mason's book went unmentioned.

Isaac Mason's birthplace, Kent County, is currently bringing public attention to him. The Kent Cultural Alliance has spearheaded preservation of a house where Mason was enslaved, a commission of his portrait and the premiere of Marlon Saunders's musical *Isaac: A Musical Journey.*

Chapter 6
RESCUES FROM SLAVE CATCHERS

HESTER NORMAN (WASHINGTON), 1847

Words make a difference. Through bias, White commentators, past and present, have called the incident of African American resistance described here the "McClintock Riot." Unlike the Jerry Rescue in Syracuse (1851) or the Oberlin-Wellington Rescue (1858), the event is not named the "Rescue of Ann Brown and Hester Norman." When the evidence is sifted, however, it is clear that John McClintock was not a pivotal figure, nor was it a "riot"— that is, public disorder without justification.

This story is about how a small but organized and engaged Black community in Pennsylvania could mobilize to rescue freedom seekers about to be returned to slavery. Free African Americans in the Carlisle area were only 2.8 percent of the total population in the county in 1850—that is, 957 individuals out of 34,327. Even so, they were ready to protect the liberty of any fellow African American against slave catchers and slave owners. The community was willing to risk its precarious position in a sometimes hostile border community. Community members were brought together by the discrimination and oppression they and their southern counterparts suffered. If necessary, they might beat an informer or provide enslaved prisoners in the jail with a rope to escape.

This tale of action on behalf of three freedom seekers is an outstanding example of agency by African Americans. It is the complementary side of the story of White abolitionists and Underground Railroad operatives. Carlisle abolitionist James Miller McKim was White, but the town's other abolitionists were all Black. As a White man, McKim felt Carlisle would not tolerate his pursuit of an abolitionist career and left, within a year becoming an agent of the American Anti-Slavery Society elsewhere.

Personal liberty laws in Pennsylvania and the periods in which they were enforceable are a crucial element of this story. Personal liberty laws were state attempts to combat enforcement of the Fugitive Slave Act of 1793. Not long before the escape of the Browns and Hester Norman, Pennsylvania's pioneering personal liberty law of 1826 had been overridden by the Supreme Court in *Prigg v. Pennsylvania* in 1842. In March 1847, a new personal liberty law was passed. Nonetheless, as far as they knew at the time of the rescue, Carlisle local officials, courts and jails could no longer ignore the Fugitive Slave Act of 1793. The Prigg decision had transferred responsibility for enforcement (or not) of the 1793 Fugitive Slave Act from the state or locality to the southern-dominated federal government. Until the viability of the new law was established, any support for freedom seekers had to come from the free Black communities in Maryland and Pennsylvania.

In Carlisle, the African American community had a series of leaders like John C. Peck, John B. Vashon and William Webb. All were barbers who ended up in Pittsburgh working for its Vigilance Committee. Until Peck left Carlisle for Pittsburgh in the early 1840s, he was a source of abolitionist literature for his barbershop clients, a leader of the short-lived Anti-Slavery Society (1834–35) and a probable Underground Railroad operative. With John B. Vashon and Richard Phillips, he established the Lay Benevolent Society in 1823, which may have helped freedom seekers. After Peck left, William Webb took over Peck's barbershop business. Ordained in the African Methodist Episcopal Church and involved in local Black organizations, Webb was still in the community at the time of the rescue—he was advertising wigs and braids in the *Carlisle Herald* on June 9, 1847. Historian Matthew Pinsker has suggested that Webb may have inherited Peck's leadership in antislavery efforts, including provision of help to freedom seekers.

Worth noting are the differences and similarities between two nearby counties figuring here, Washington County, Maryland, and Cumberland County, Pennsylvania. Although separated by the Mason-Dixon line, South Central Pennsylvania was much like Washington County. It was fertile and produced grain, and it had a similar ethnic makeup of Germans, African Americans (mostly free) and people of English descent.

Unlike the Quaker-dominated areas of Pennsylvania, Cumberland County was not known for being antislavery, although some German churches were against slaveholding. Carlisle, in Cumberland County, was home to Dickinson College and Carlisle Barracks, a cavalry training school for the U.S. Army. Both brought in southerners.

Hagerstown in Western Maryland was known for its slave catchers and slave trade but not for a large enslaved population. Hagerstown's White residents reacted vociferously to escaping bondsmen, a problem not helped by Washington County's location near the Pennsylvania border. An 1850 article in the *Herald of Freedom and Torch Light* claimed that the county, which had 2,090 enslaved African Americans, lost $10,000 a year in the form of escaping bondsmen.

White Hagerstown viewed freedom seekers as absconders. It considered abolitionists to have poisoned their minds with a notion that they would find freedom and equality in the North. Slave owners, according to the *Hagerstown Freeman*, believed that the absconders would in fact "have liberty to starve." They would soon wish for their former situation with "a kind master and a happy home."

In early summer of 1847, Hester (Esther) Norman, Lloyd Brown and Brown's ten-year-old daughter Ann seized an opportunity to join twelve freedom seekers in what southerners called a "stampede." Lloyd was prepared because an unidentified sympathizer in Hagerstown had given him a list of safe roads and houses for the journey. Following the Cumberland Valley, the freedom seekers crossed the Mason-Dixon line. They headed toward Carlisle in Cumberland County, Pennsylvania, over fifty miles from Hagerstown. Carlisle, like Chambersburg and Shippensburg, was on the way north for those fleeing from or through Washington County.

Lloyd and Ann Brown and Hester Norman were fleeing James H. Kennedy and his father-in-law, Jacob Hollingsworth. Jacob was known as Colonel Hollingsworth because of his rank in the Maryland militia. He had owned a Washington County estate, Fountain Rock, but had sold it to invest in a sugar plantation near New Orleans. He still owned the house in Hagerstown where he lived. Kennedy, the son of a successful merchant, was himself a Hagerstown merchant. For slaveholders like Kennedy and Hollingsworth, the freedom seekers represented a sizeable investment.

Kennedy and Hollingsworth seemed to be clueless about the bondsmen's motives for escape. Hollingsworth later testified that he considered Hester to be "perfectly happy and reconciled to her situation" and "treated with the greatest kindness." He did not take into consideration that Hester's husband,

Jacob Hollingsworth's house is shown on the left in its current disrepair. *Jenny Masur*.

George Norman, a skilled mason, had protected his freedom by moving to Carlisle. Hollingsworth did not realize that the convenience of having a house on a major thoroughfare not only applied to him—it also facilitated Lloyd and Ann's escape.

Hollingsworth had given Hester to James Kennedy. She served as a nursemaid, an irksome, twenty-four-hour-a-day job, in which she would suffer consequences for the Kennedy children's misbehavior. Hollingsworth had no qualms about also giving Kennedy a ten-year-old girl, Ann, the daughter of his longtime carriage driver Lloyd Brown. The gift had to have distressed Lloyd.

Within days of the triple escape in the early summer of 1847, Colonel Hollingsworth authorized his lawyer son George Howard Hollingsworth to join Kennedy on the trip to recapture Lloyd, Ann and Hester. In hot pursuit, Kennedy and Howard Hollingsworth caught up to them on a road in Shippensburg near Carlisle. The freedom seekers were in luck, however, as Samuel Taylor was passing by. He was a local White wagonmaker and an equality-minded Methodist. Although outnumbered and armed with only a stake, Taylor fearlessly stopped the pursuers until the three freedom seekers could run away. The three sought refuge with an African American named Charles Marshall in Carlisle. On the morning of June 2, 1847, Kennedy and several deputies barged into Marshall's home. They seized the freedom seekers in order to arrest them and took them to appear before Justice of the Peace Smith.

The justice of the peace accepted the oral identification of the three bondsmen as proof of ownership by Kennedy and Hollingsworth. Justice Smith issued a warrant for the arrest of Lloyd, Ann and Hester as specified by the Fugitive Slave Act of 1793. Smith also issued a certificate of removal allowing the owners to take the captives back to slavery in Maryland immediately. For whatever reason, Lloyd acknowledged his enslaved status.

The slave owners and posse did not invade Marshall's home without consequences. With Charles jailed, a "spinster," Rachel Marshall (probably Charles's sister), bravely filed a complaint on Charles's behalf charging forcible entry into the Marshall home. A warrant was issued for the intruders. That meant that before leaving for Maryland, Hollingsworth and Kennedy needed to arrange bail. So that they could do so, the county jailor agreed to hold the bondsmen in the jail as a favor—an illegal one, as it turned out. Smith ordered the captives to be committed to jail.

Two African American townspeople, John Clellans and Clara Jones, saw the slave catchers on the way to the jail and spread the word. Blacks, especially women, began to gather near the jail. When Hester's husband, George, made an attempt to rescue Hester, the burly sheriff's assistant Robert McCartney threw George against the jail wall and threatened to shoot him. Although the crowd had sticks or other missiles readily at hand, the three freedom seekers were safely jailed. The crowd worried the sheriff, however, and he quickly deputized five extra men. The first attempt at rescue had failed.

Judge Samuel Hepburn presided over the lower court hearing of the Carlisle rescuers. *Cumberland County Historical Society.*

Meanwhile, persons unknown had time to hire Samuel Adair, a local attorney, to represent the freedom seekers. Thanks to Adair, at noon, a writ of habeas corpus was issued questioning the sheriff's custody of Ann, Lloyd and Hester. A court appearance of the freedom seekers was set for four o'clock. African Americans began to gather at the courthouse.

After he arrived at the courthouse, Judge Samuel Hepburn recognized the morning's certificate of removal as legal. He then addressed the writ of habeas corpus, focusing on Sheriff Jacob Hoffer's authority to hold the freedom seekers. The judge decided that Justice Smith should not have committed them to jail and legally turned the three over to their alleged owners. Hollingsworth and Kennedy couldn't act on the remand, however. They had left when the judge made his decision about the sheriff's prior imprisonment of the freedom seekers. Even though the judge granted the owners habeas corpus—that is, control over the freedom seekers—at that moment, the owners were not present to take custody of the enslaved prisoners.

During the hearing, African American men and women gathered in and about the courthouse. They were ready to use force if necessary to prevent the return of Hester, Ann and Lloyd. The angry crowd must have noticed the departure of the slave catchers from the courthouse and decided to take advantage of it. With determination, men and women climbed the stairs and pushed into the courtroom. Several men rushed up the courtroom aisles toward the prisoners although the judge was still on the bench.

Because Kennedy and Hollingsworth had asked the sheriff to watch the prisoners while the slave catchers were gone, the sheriff and his backup stuck close to the prisoners' box, blocking the rescuers from the prisoners. White witnesses later identified participants in the attempted rescue. John Clellans approached the prisoners' box with what appeared to be a sharp weapon, but a deputy hit Clellans on the head. Augustus Coates grabbed the arm of a deputy. Meanwhile, John Garver urged the freedom seekers to flee.

The sheriff, deputies and bystanders resisted the rescuers. Either the jailor or a deputy drew a gun, threatening anyone approaching the prisoners' box. The

Left: James McClintock was devastated by his trial and the blame he received for Hester's rescue and Kennedy's death. *Archives and Special Collections, Dickinson College.*

Above: Members of a crowd rally to rescue a captured freedom seeker. *Wallach Division Picture Collection, New York Public Library.*

judge ordered the courtroom cleared. The constables and officers of the court locked the prisoners in the courthouse, holding them in a temporary prison in violation of the new 1847 law. The second rescue attempt was squelched.

Dickinson College professor John McClintock passed by the courthouse just as the judge was ruling on habeas corpus. Informed of proceedings related to "fugitive slaves," McClintock entered the courthouse to investigate. McClintock listened briefly until the judge had finished. McClintock then privately raised the existence of a new Pennsylvania personal liberty law to the judge and the defense lawyer.

It was news to the judge that this law, passed only months before, again made it illegal for local authorities to jail alleged fugitives or to issue a certificate of removal for them after satisfactory identification. As the judge cleared the courtroom, McClintock went home to get his copy of the law. He later remembered, "There was a melee in the courtroom, the nature of which I did not understand." What he disregarded was the second rescue attempt.

When the slave owners returned from posting bail, they had a two-horse carriage waiting at the courthouse door, ready to return to Maryland. What an article in *The Liberator* called "a large portion of the [local] colored population" was ready to stop them, regardless of risk, once the court reopened its doors. It was incontrovertible, said McClintock's biographer, that "the blacks had shown a disposition to unite for a rescue all through the day, and that they were in no need of instigation."

As Kennedy and Hollingsworth took Hester, Lloyd and Ann to the waiting carriage, the crowd surged toward the slave catchers. McClintock, a bystander, wrote in his diary that "blows were struck…by the white men first." Carlisle's *American Volunteer* of June 10, 1847, reported: "A frightful melee ensued in the street, in which for some minutes paving stones were hurled in showers, and clubs and arms used with painful effect." Witnesses would identify John Clellans, Moses Garver, George Coates, Anthony Boon and George Norman as leaders, and all would go to prison. Most Whites present did not interfere, for they considered the return of the freedom seekers to slavery to be legitimate.

Hollingsworth and Kennedy were able to get the freedom seekers into the vehicle. Nonetheless, they could not stop either Hester's rescue by George Norman or Ann's by some Black women. That left Lloyd in the carriage to be sent back to jail in Hagerstown and possible sale to the Deep South.

The rescuers with Ann and Hester ran off in the direction of the Market House. Kennedy, age thirty, was strong and six feet tall, but he made a near-fatal mistake by following. Someone in the crowd threw debris at him. When Kennedy fell or tripped, crowd members attacked or trampled him in their rush. He suffered a knife wound, a blow to the head and damage to his kneecap.

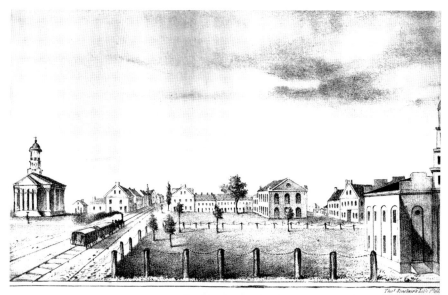

Public Square in Carlisle.

Carlisle Public Square, site of the rescue, was shown in Sherman Day's 1843 *Historical Collections of Pennsylvania. Cumberland Historical Society.*

Protectors continued to hustle Hester and Ann down a nearby alley. The two were thrust into the cellar of the Snodgrass family's store. Susan Hunter closed the cellar door and placed herself on it. Ann and Hester had eluded the pursuers. The hearing and the rescue lasted less than two hours.

Hester and Ann spent days passing from safe house to safe house. They went first to African American Richard Johnston's house and then to the cellar of African American James Jones, the head waiter at the Winrott Tavern. Sympathizers sent the woman and girl on to Harrisburg, after which they disappeared.

Attention now shifted to McClintock because of his stature at the college and his antislavery stance in a proslavery town. The public and the authorities presumed him guilty of instigation. By nighttime, the atmosphere in town was tense.

The consequences for bystander McClintock and those considered "rioters" soon overshadowed Hester and Ann's escape. Carlisle's *American Volunteer* would write that the African Americans had to have been "duped by a few Abolition agents." The authorities acted quickly, indicting one White "abolitionist" professor and thirty-five Blacks (including nine women). In the rescue of Hester and Ann, charges were:

> *First, for riot and breach of the peace; second, for riotously assembling with the intention of breaching the peace, and for the additional purposes of rescuing three fugitive slaves then peaceably and lawfully in the possession of their owners; and the third, for assault and battery.*

Unlike McClintock, who was set at liberty because of $300 posted for bail, the African Americans were jailed from June until the August 25 trial.

The incident became a cause célèbre. Newspapers up and down the East Coast, as well as those on the Pennsylvania-Maryland border, reported on the event. Carlisle, indeed Hagerstown and the whole South, needed a scapegoat. Many in Carlisle felt the town had been disgraced. When James Kennedy died on June 25, residents blamed it on his injuries in the rescue. They honored Kennedy's body by following it to the train to Hagerstown and by sending their regrets to the new widow.

In Hagerstown, people were indignant. Using the occasion of Kennedy's death, Hagerstown held a public meeting. Those attending appointed committees to appeal for redress from what they called "the authorities," the Maryland legislature and Congress.

On August 25, 1847, the Carlisle case was presented in the Quarter Sessions Court of Cumberland County. Blacks and Whites were tried together. There were too many defendants to fit into the prisoners' box. Packing the courtroom, an excited crowd, drawn from a range of society, was eager to follow the proceedings.

Adair appeared again for the African American defendants thanks to McClintock, who included seventy dollars for Adair in his total legal costs. Thirty-six witnesses were called to cast McClintock as the instigator to riot and the Blacks as rioters. However, muddled testimony did not permit the prosecution to refute the defense or to overcome the aura of respect for the brilliant young Professor McClintock.

The defense convinced the court of McClintock's innocence, and McClintock was acquitted. Many, but not all, of the African American defendants were also acquitted, thanks perhaps to Jacob Rheem, who came forth as a witness on behalf of them and McClintock. Rheem was a major White community figure, a dedicated Methodist (serving as leader for the African American class of his church), a borough council president and a real estate broker.

Because the presiding judge, Samuel Hepburn, had been the one to remand Lloyd, Hester and Ann to Hollingsworth and Kennedy, Hepburn was not neutral. When the jury found only thirteen of the Blacks guilty of rioting and found McClintock innocent, the judge protested angrily. He declared that in a civil case, he would have requested a retrial. His protest amazed all who knew legal etiquette.

Judge Hepburn sentenced two African American defendants to the county jail for ten days and for six months, respectively. More harshly, he sentenced the other eleven African Americans to solitary confinement and hard labor for three years at Eastern State Penitentiary in Philadelphia. The eleven most notably included Hester's husband, George. The *Baltimore Sun*'s transcripts of the testimony at the trial listed the others: Valentine Thomas, John Clellans, Augustus Coates, John Gray, Anthony Boon, Charles Turner, Jacob Garver, Moses Jones, Achilles Vandergrift and Henry Myers.

These eleven defendants were lucky that McClintock remained involved. He hired a sharp Philadelphia lawyer, Charles Gibbons. In April 1848, Gibbons filed a writ of error with the state supreme court. He used the grounds that the sentence was overly severe for a misdemeanor charge. During quarter sessions court, the state supreme court met on the case in Harrisburg, the state capital.

George Norman was imprisoned in the Eastern State Penitentiary, Philadelphia, shown here in about 1831. *Collection of the Eastern State Penitentiary Historic Site.*

The supreme court justices reversed the lower court's decision. They ruled that the freedom seekers should have been able to leave the Carlisle courtroom freely. The justices decreed three-quarters of a year at the penitentiary to be the equivalent of two years in the county jail. The Carlisle prisoners were released on June 6, 1848, about a year after the rescue and nine months after entering the penitentiary. Notably, other such sentences had not been reviewed by a higher court. If the ruling had been applied to other cases, more prisoners in the penitentiary who had received harsh sentences for rioting would have been released.

The rescue can be analyzed in regard to the 1847 personal liberty law or as a case of border conflict. Historian Jennifer Coval, however, makes an important point: "The human voice and spirit that was at the heart of the slavery issue sometimes becomes obscured in the study of the antebellum period." It is important to consider the courage and intentions of all those, White and Black, involved in the rescue. For abolitionists and Carlisle's African American community, the rescue was a success. Results of the hearing in the supreme court were a vindication.

The rescue reflects how precious freedom and family reunification were to members of an African American border community composed of a mixture of free people and freedom seekers. Blacks in Carlisle identified with Hester, Lloyd and Ann, who faced crises of freedom and family. Women especially are mentioned over and over again in newspaper accounts as rescuers and observers at the trials.

Jennifer Coval is again insightful when she analyzes the costs incurred by the African American community for the risks taken and the bravery shown during the rescue. George Norman's loyalty to his wife cost him nine months in the penitentiary. Ann and Hester's freedom exacted a price from Carlisle's entire Black community, despite the fact that not all defendants were convicted and those in the penitentiary were released. There was harassment during searches for Hester, Ann and the rescuers. Participants suffered injuries during the melee. The small community lost the contributions of thirty-four able-bodied members for varying amounts of time. Nine women were in jail from June to August. Eleven African Americans, described by a newspaper as "many of them men of families and respectability," were sentenced to three years of labor and solitary confinement. In addition to their suffering, they could not make their usual contributions to the community.

This instance of the rescue of Ann and Hester, nevertheless, was not the only time Carlisle African Americans put their lives and livelihoods at risk. Look at other risks taken before or after by some of those imprisoned: John Clellans, active in the attempted courtroom rescue, was only twenty-one but had already served time for rioting, from 1845 to 1847. Despite inadequate proof and a possible countersuit, in 1850, Moses Jones was accused of being a "fugitive slave." George Norman was not the only one inspired by the memories of a slave state. His fellow southerners, whether or not formerly enslaved, were Anthony Boon, Valentine Thomas, Henry Meyers and Augustus Coates from Maryland, Charles Turner and Moses Jones from Virginia and John Gray from the District of Columbia.

Neither Whites nor Blacks could afford the consequences of this rescue, yet they acted. The consequences the African Americans faced were more dire—jail or penitentiary for those free by birth or manumission, or a return to slavery with harsh punishment or sale south for freedom seekers. There were three attempts at rescue. As historians Matthew Pinsker and Cooper Wingert point out, it cannot be coincidental that Charles Marshall offered shelter, Rachel Marshall lodged a complaint, Black men and women appeared by the jail and the courthouse or that someone hired lawyer Adair.

McClintock left a diary and other records of his thoughts and feelings about the rescue and its impact. Carlisle's African Americans left no written record. To understand the intensity of the unity with Lloyd, Ann and Hester felt by Carlisle's African Americans, it is necessary to heed Susan Hunter's words. She was the wife of John Hunter, a probable Underground Railroad agent, and part of the group of women rescuing Ann and Hester. At the first trial of the rescuers, a witness testified he had heard Susan Hunter say that she would fight, "Yes! bless God, up to my knees in blood for my color."

James Hamlet (Baltimore County), 1850

It was James Hamlet from Baltimore who had the misfortune to be the first arrested under the Fugitive Slave Act of 1850. On September 26, 1850, eight days after President Millard Fillmore signed the act into law, the New York City fugitive slave commissioner issued a warrant for Hamlet's arrest at the request of his owner's agent. Marshals promptly arrested Hamlet.

The new Fugitive Slave Act was an essential part of the Compromise of 1850, designed to appease the South. In the North, as the first implementation of the new act, Hamlet's arrest created commotion among White abolitionists and all African Americans. Hamlet's heartbreaking capture led to calls to action and repudiation of the Fugitive Slave Act. It caused flight among many freedom seekers well-established in the North while those who remained behind armed themselves.

Opponents of the act agreed that those escaping slavery were not fugitives from justice; nor did they think every citizen should be obliged to cooperate in the return of freedom seekers. African Americans were outraged. Indeed, the new law and its implementation, although not a complete surprise, would spark an explosive reaction from Black communities all over the Northeast and Midwest. Indignation stimulated responses in word and deed. Escapes from slavery seemed to increase, while those seeking to speed the freedom seekers on their way became more militant.

Black abolitionists made themselves known outside the African American community. African Americans in New York City were quick to react. It is significant that those who organized and spoke at Black protest meetings were ministers of the African American churches that were key institutions in the Black community; professionals who, by their positions, were prominent in that community; and individuals associated with slavery by birth, kinship or friendship.

James Hamlet was, according to newspaper descriptions, "a light mulatto," about twenty-eight years old. Maryland documents added that he had a scar on one cheek. He was raised in Baltimore County but had made Williamsburgh in Brooklyn his home. He had been living and working as a free man in New York City for about two years.

When he appeared in an 1850 census in Brooklyn (taken June 1) under the name of James Williams, he was living in the household of a Mrs. Francis. He had married Harriet, a woman from Maryland. Their marriage had occurred while they were still in Maryland, judging from the ages and places of birth of their children. James and Harriet were parents of three children—Catherine, age five, and Elijah, age three, both born in Maryland, and baby Alvord, born in New York. For a couple years, Hamlet worked for and lived with Silas Wood, a builder. By 1850, Hamlet was working as a porter at a store belonging to Tilton & Maloney on Water Street. He was member of the African Methodist Episcopal Zion Church. The *Independent* newspaper reported that he had a reputation "as a sober, industrious, intelligent and trust-worthy [*sic*] man," all values appealing to the audience courted by abolitionists in the fight against slavery.

One Saturday, Hamlet had been working as usual when United States deputy marshals appeared with a warrant in hand. They whisked him off to city hall, ostensibly to be a witness in a theft case. Hamlet's fellow African Americans had been prepared for the first enforcement of the 1850 act. When arrested, Hamlet signaled to nearby African American observers, perhaps using a secret sign. At the first suggestion of opposition, though, the deputy marshals pulled out revolvers, while the police stood by as reinforcements. Having quashed the possibility of a rescue, the marshals rushed Hamlet off. The deputy marshals in the neighborhood of the United States commissioner's office misled the Blacks waiting there. Throngs of Blacks later mistakenly gathered at the New York City jail known as the Tombs.

When Hamlet arrived at city hall, he was hauled to a hearing before federal commissioner Alexander Gardiner. Gardiner was newly appointed to oversee New York City claims under the Fugitive Slave Act of 1850. The commissioner had the power to determine the status of the purported "slave" after hearing from the claimant to ownership and his witnesses. The commissioner was biased by the fees—ten dollars per pronouncement as enslaved and five dollars per pronouncement as free.

The first hearing under the Fugitive Slave Act was held in front of a restricted audience on the very Saturday of Hamlet's capture. Hamlet was quickly identified as the bondsman of Mary Brown of Baltimore by her son Gustavus and the husband of her daughter Eliza Jane, Thomas

J. Clare. Gustavus was a clerk to E.M. Fenby in New York City and Clare an employee of a shot-manufacturing company in Baltimore. The two stated that while working for that shot company, Hamlet had escaped two years before. Testimony said that he had left by "concealing himself on a burden [freight] train on the railroad between this city and Philadelphia, unbeknownst to the conductors."

Gustavus testified that he had known Hamlet since his own childhood and, indeed, Hamlet appeared as a nine-year-old boy in the 1831 inventory of James G. Brown, Mary Brown's deceased husband. Before living in New York, Gustavus had been living with his mother on Hanover Street in Baltimore when Hamlet ran away. Gustavus had glimpsed Hamlet several times in New York and informed his mother. She had awaited passage of the new Fugitive Slave Act before acting.

Thomas J. Clare, the son-in-law who had power of attorney, had masterminded the recapture. He had married into the family seventeen years before and had known Hamlet about twenty years. On cross-examination, he testified that he had responsibility for assigning Hamlet jobs when Hamlet was not doing "work about the [Browns'] house." Clare hired Hamlet out on occasion—for example, as a drayman, or at the time of his escape, to the shot-making concern where Clare worked. The dangerous fumes and the heavy work of shot-making could have been the immediate motivation for Hamlet to flee.

Besides their sworn testimony, Gustavus and Clare produced a copy of the will passing ownership of James Hamlet from James G. Brown to his widow, Mary Brown. Although Hamlet protested that he was born to a free woman, he was neither given the opportunity to testify on his own behalf nor allowed the rights to habeas corpus, a jury trial or presentation of his own witnesses. The defense of Hamlet consisted of a quick intervention by a New York defense lawyer named Asa Child, a former attorney general of Connecticut and friend of Hamlet's former employer Silas Wood. Child missed part of the hearing but cross-examined the witnesses and declared himself content with the proceedings.

Commissioner Gardiner signed the necessary certificate that declared Hamlet to be a "fugitive slave" based on physical identification and proof of ownership. Gardiner then provided the warrant ordering Hamlet's return to Mary Brown. Hamlet was left to rue the day that his grandmother lost his freedom papers and those of his parents. Because the representatives of Mary Brown feared an attempt at rescue, they requested and received additional protection. Meanwhile, Hamlet's wife knew nothing of his arrest

The Phoenix Shot Tower where James Hamlet worked still stands in Baltimore. *Enoch Pratt Free Library, Maryland's State Library Resource Center.*

THE FUGITIVE SLAVE LAW.....HAMLET IN CHAINS.

The *National Anti-Slavery Standard*, October 17, 1850. *B326.5 N213, Rare Book & Manuscript Library, Columbia University in the City of New York.*

and seizure. Indeed, reports mistakenly claimed that she died of grief on hearing the news.

It was too late by the time a member of the New York Vigilance Committee, Reverend Charles Ray, and an abolitionist only identified as Benton arrived. The authorities were handcuffing Hamlet and handing him over to the deputy United States marshal accompanying him to Baltimore. The deputy marshal, deemed necessary in case of trouble, bustled Hamlet into a waiting carriage. The carriage drove rapidly to the wharf, and in its wake, a crowd yelled threats against the officials and slaveholders. Curses flew, directed at the lawmakers responsible for the Fugitive Slave Act. At the wharf, representatives of Graham, Potee & McKinley, a so-called police firm, led Hamlet onto the first available steamboat to Baltimore, the *John Potter* of the Camden and Amboy Line.

Within three hours of his arrest, Hamlet found himself back in Baltimore. Hamlet was probably still in shock when the captors handed him over to the well-known slave trader Joseph S. Donovan. Donovan promptly set a price of $800 for Hamlet. For the foreseeable future, Hamlet was a piece of merchandise in a slave pen. The deputy marshal, Benjamin Tallmadge, efficiently telegraphed the news of his completed assignment to his father, the marshal Henry F. Tallmadge. It was a smooth first implementation of the new Fugitive Slave Act, all financed by $71 dollars in federal taxes.

In response, influential members of New York's African American community united to form the Committee of Thirteen to fight the Fugitive Slave Act. They intended to help those in flight from slavery and emphasize the increased risk of kidnapping to freedom seekers and free Blacks alike. The secret membership of the Committee of Thirteen was spread across a broad spectrum of society—educator and journalist Junius C. Morel, physician James McCune Smith, publisher Philip Bell and restaurateurs George and Thomas Downing. This informal committee included members from the original New York Committee of Vigilance and operatives of the Underground Railroad. It was chaired by John J. Zuille, an activist in the Black convention movement. The committee relied on donations to help freedom seekers who came to them through word of mouth.

The Committee of Thirteen urgently mobilized to protest both the treatment of Hamlet and the risks for other African Americans. The committee signed the handbill announcing the first mass meeting at Zion Chapel on the Tuesday after Hamlet's arrest. It and following meetings were occasions to join in opposition to, and denunciation of, the new Fugitive Slave Act.

DR. JAMES McCUNE SMITH.

Dr. James McCune Smith, born in Manhattan, received his medical degree at the University of Glasgow. *Schomburg Center for Research in Black Culture*.

Although the immediate motive of the meeting at Zion Chapel was to raise $800 for Hamlet's freedom, the organizers used the occasion for a rally against the Fugitive Slave Act. The handbill announcing the meeting was a call to action, referring not only to "the panting slave!" but also to "freemen to be made slaves!" The handbill proclaimed: "Your Fire-side is in danger of being invaded! Devote this night to the question of YOUR DUTY in the CRISIS." It asked, "Shall we defend our liberties?"

The handbill stimulated a good turnout. The meeting more than filled Zion Chapel's 1,500 seats. There was a sprinkling of Whites, but two-thirds of the audience were Black women. A who's who of African American community and antislavery leaders in New York led the meeting. There were twenty vice presidents, including Dr. James McCune Smith, the first university-trained African American physician and the founder of the New York City Abolition Society; Reverend Samuel Cornish, a Presbyterian minister and member of the New York Vigilance Committee; and Reverend J.T. Raymond, founder of the New York Zion Baptist Church and an antislavery activist since the 1830s. The meeting president was William Powell, founder of the Manhattan Anti-Slavery Society and owner of the Colored Seamen's Boarding House.

The format of the meeting was not unusual: election of officers, passionate speeches and passage of enthusiastic resolutions. It was the vehemence and determination of speakers and their insistence on action that were exceptional.

Meeting president William Powell's initial plea was a call to action, referring to "the blood-thirsty slaveholder" and "the black-hearted, villainous kidnapper" ready to seize members of the audience. Powell began, "Let us be united as one man, regarding our first rights as inherent and inalienable.... Ye are told to submit peaceably to the laws. Will you do so?" Denunciations of the "covenant of death, and agreement with hell" flew from speakers' mouths as they warned of the entrapment and kidnapping legitimated by the act. When asked if those present would submit to enforcement, the audience repeatedly roared, "No! no!" Powell urged: "Let us be united as one man. Ye are men with arms in your hands. Will you not defend your helpless brethren, or will you let them die? Defend them—defend them." He next asked, "Shall we…tamely submit…our limbs to the shackles, and clank our chains to the sweet music of passive obedience?" Punctuated by hisses and cries of "Shame!," Hiram Wilson read the offending law. Speakers repudiated it, despite stating their desire to be "good law-abiding *citizens*." One resolve declared it to be "far better that a thousand lives perish in the rescue, than that a single human being be permitted to be dragged from our midst into hopeless bondage."

Abolitionist lawyer Alanson Nash's letter, which was read to the crowd, detailed illegal aspects of the act as specific as denial of citizenship to a child born in a free state or to a bondsman brought into a free state by an owner. Nonetheless, a letter from the Radical Republican lawyer and congressman Thaddeus Stevens warned from Washington, "I Can [*sic*] give but little hope that the infamous Slave Law will be declared unconstitutional."

The climax to the rousing speeches was an oath by George T. Downing. He would defend "the panting slave" and his own life, home and family with violence if necessary. He swore, "If any fiend in human shape—dare cross the threshold of my castle, I will send him to h-ll before he shall accomplish his mission." He urged freedom seekers to heed Patrick Henry and George Washington and "arm themselves with the surest and most deadly weapons… to resist unto death." John S. Jacobs from North Carolina identified himself as a freedom seeker and chimed in to cheers, "I am an American citizen." He exhorted the audience to, under the present law, "let them only take your dead bodies."

The final note was optimistic. To great cheers, Reverend Charles T. Ray announced that donors had raised the necessary $800. It was "near midnight" when, as the *Evening Post* of October 2, 1850, put it, "the assembly adjourned in great excitement." Five hours had passed.

One African American, Isaac Hollenbeck, a worker on the Troy and Erie Railroad, had pledged an astounding sum of $100. Surprisingly, however, most donors were neither African Americans nor White abolitionists. The *Journal of Commerce* raised the bulk of the money from city merchants who discreetly held views supporting slavery because of economic ties to southern interests.

The perspective of most New York City merchants soon became obvious when they established the Union Safety Committee at their own public meeting. What historian Eric Foner called "a kind of Vigilance Committee in reverse" saw purchases of freedom as a means to recognize slaveholders' rights yet promote gradual, legal emancipation. Usually, the merchants' generosity was directed toward redemption of bondsmen on the condition that they leave the country.

Many abolitionists, on the other hand, saw paying to redeem Hamlet's freedom differently, especially since he had already been living in freedom. Payment was a moral issue and only justified to protect a freedom seeker's security. Payment let slaveholders name freedom's price and helped them profit from slavery.

John H. Woodgate, a prosperous merchant with contacts in Baltimore, volunteered to be go-between. He went to Baltimore to make arrangements with Mary Brown and the slave dealer. "James Hamlett" was manumitted in Maryland on October 4.

From the day of Hamlet's arrest to his manumission, only about one week passed, but that week was filled with heartbreak, calls to action and repudiation of the Fugitive Slave Act. In one short weekend, Hamlet went from the degradation of slavery and potential auction back to freedom. What newspapers politely referred to as the widespread "excitement" of Black New Yorkers culminated in great joy at Hamlet's deliverance.

19

Richard R. Battie
Witness —

On this 2d day of October 1850, before me Clerk of Baltimore County Court personally appears Richard R. Battie and makes oath on the Holy Evangely of Almighty God, that Maria Davis, aged thirty one years, of yellow complexion, five feet two inches high, has a scar on the left cheek bone, is the identical person manumitted by a certain Michael ... by deed recorded in Liber R.M.B. No. 81 folio one of the chattel Records of Baltimore County, and that said Maria Davis was raised in Baltimore County

Maria Davis
and State of Maryland. —

A. W. Bradford Clk

Thomas I. Clare
(Union Square
West ... St.)
Witness

On this 4th day of October 1850, before me, Clerk of Baltimore County Court, personally appears Thomas I. Clare and makes oath on the Holy Evangely of Almighty God, that James Hamlett, aged twenty eight years, of light complexion, five feet six and a half inches in height, has a scar on the left side of the neck, is the identical person manumitted by Mary Brown, in and by deed of manumission of this day, recorded in Liber A.W.B. No. 81 folio ... one of the chattel Records

James Hamlett
(Balt. County)
of Baltimore County, and that the said James was raised in Baltimore County and State of Maryland

George H. Hoeh
Witness

Polly or Mary Dowden

On this 7th day of October 1850 before me Clerk of Baltimore County Court personally appears Geo. H. Hoeh and makes oath on the Holy Evangely of Almighty God that Polly or Mary Dowden aged about 25 years, of yellow complexion five feet one inch high has no scars or left shoulder is the identical person manumitted by deponent by deed of manumission bearing date October 5th 1850 and recorded in Liber A.W.B. No. 81 folio — one of the chattel Records of Baltimore County and that the said Polly or Mary Dowden was raised in Harford & Baltimore Counties and State of Maryland.

A. W. Bradford Clk

A state-issued manumission certificate made official the redemption of James Hamlet from slavery. *Collection of the Maryland State Archives.*

City Hall.

A large crowd gathered in New York City Hall Park to welcome James Hamlet back. *Wallach Division Picture Collection, New York Public Library.*

Even though Hamlet did not stay long at the slave pen, those days until he was legally manumitted must have been traumatic. They were filled with anxiety about a future in slavery separated from his family. He spent hours witnessing heart-wrenching scenes of other families sold and forced to undergo that very fate. He was immersed in an atmosphere in which he shared despair and desperation with all around him.

All that changed with Woodgate's arrival with glad news and the money to redeem Hamlet's freedom. Woodgate accompanied him back to New York City. On Saturday, October 5, Hamlet arrived at City Hall Park at noon. He found several thousand supporters, African American and White, gathered there to exult at his triumphant return. The crowd greeted Hamlet and Woodgate with joyous cheers.

Called by the Committee of Thirteen, the meeting again featured the broad support of leaders of the New York Black abolitionist community in favor of Hamlet and against the Fugitive Slave Act. Significant Underground Railroad entities were represented by Reverend Charles Ray of the New York Vigilance Committee, Louis Napoleon of the American Anti-Slavery Society Office and Jacob Gibbs, an operative. The choice of meeting officers was telling, with Reverend John P. Thompson as the president. Louis Napoleon, Dr. James McCune Smith, William C. Innis and Albro Lyons were vice presidents. William Powell was secretary.

The crowd was enthusiastic. The meeting opened with a prayer by Reverend John Thompson and the reading of resolutions on Hamlet's illegal arrest and the unconstitutional Fugitive Slave Act. William P. Powell reminded those present of the reason for the occasion. The hero of the hour was introduced:

You now see JAMES HAMLET before you, redeemed, regenerated, disenthralled, not by the universal genius of emancipation but by the universal genius of the almighty [Yankee] dollar. We are here to sympathize with him, because in his person American Liberty has been struck down: and thank God he stands here as a resurrection of a better day…I welcome you JAMES HAMLET.

It was a touching scene. Hamlet shed tears. Many reached for Hamlet's hands, also crying. To end this outburst of emotion, to the sound of resounding cheers, Reverend John J. Thompson, a Black Methodist, stepped up with James Hamlet and spoke movingly:

I am partially blind…and yet I see JAMES HAMLET whose hand I hold. Yesterday he was a chattel; today he is a man.…Thank God there is a conscience in this and other cities of the Union that will yet wipe that [Fugitive Slave] bill from the statute-book.…I beseech you, HAMLET, take not flight to Canada nor hide in the woods, but if you are to perish, perish here…(Great cheering)

While Hamlet was too overcome to speak, organizers presented his wife and children to share in the audience's kisses, hugs and tears. Speakers offered thanks to God, the donors of the redemption money and the mayor for giving permission to use the steps of city hall. To cheers, the mayor of New York City, Caleb Woodhull, promised that the police would not cooperate with capture of freedom seekers.

The meeting was over. The *National Anti-Slavery Standard* reported that many in the audience joined in the song "Come All Who Claim the Freeman's Name." There arose the shout, "Rejoice, my people!" Supporters triumphantly carried Hamlet off on their shoulders, stopping at the *Journal of Commerce* office to give three cheers three times over. Hundreds escorted Hamlet to the Williamsburgh Ferry. Many continued back with Hamlet to Hamlet's neighborhood, also the home of other freedom seekers.

On October 9, Williamsburgh hosted its own ceremony in the African American Congregational church of Reverend Simeon Jocelyn. Reverend Jocelyn was the White minister famed as proponent of the first college for African Americans and founder of a Connecticut antislavery society. Robert Hamilton of Williamsburg welcomed Hamlet back. Hamlet had the opportunity to tell his own story of arrest, loss of freedom and incarceration in the slave pen. He called for heavenly retribution for Mary

Brown, who claimed him, and for President Millard Fillmore, who signed the Fugitive Slave Act. Hamlet cried when hearing a speaker at the meeting detail slavery's hellish nature, his memories of enslavement revived. The *New York Tribune* reported that Reverend Jocelyn closed the meeting by making "some pointed resolutions…unanimously adopted" repudiating "the atrocious Fugitive Slave bill." In Brooklyn, in order to help freedom seekers, abolitionists formed a Committee of Nine, and in Williamsburgh itself, they established a Committee of Five.

Lewis Tappan was an active abolitionist and a generous donor to the cause. *Library of Congress.*

After these meetings, little is known of James Hamlet. He may have started using the name James Williams again as he had in the 1850 census, either for security's sake or because his original name was James Hamilton Williams, as the *Independent* stated in October 1850. James Williams, a porter, appears in the 1856 and 1857 Brooklyn city directories. There is no listing for the 1860s. The 1870 Federal Census shows James Williams, Black janitor and porter, age fifty. Williams was living in New York City (Ward 3, District 5) with a spouse, Harriet, age forty, both of whom were born in Maryland.

Hamlet's tribulations had widely felt consequences. Newspapers across the North and South picked up the story. For those against slavery, Hamlet's story was a triumph over the Fugitive Slave Act, and for those who were proslavery, it was a setback. A pamphlet about the Fugitive Slave Act memorialized Hamlet's capture and redemption. It was headed "Civil Liberty Outraged" and written by prominent abolitionist Lewis Tappan. The American and Foreign Anti-Slavery Society quickly published it in 1850. Tappan used Hamlet's story to build sympathy for the "panting fugitive," to illustrate the wider issue of the unconstitutional nature of the law and to recommend to freedom seekers that they stand their ground in the United States (albeit with discretion). The pamphlet sold thirteen thousand copies in three weeks. As a result, 1,600 people signed a pledge of disobedience to the law. James Hamlet's arrest opened a decade of resistance.

CONCLUSION

Regardless of where it was or is, the institution of slavery imposed and imposes unacceptable conditions on human beings. Wherever and whenever there is slavery, there is always resistance through flight. The value of examining the Underground Railroad never diminishes. The pursuit of freedom is never finished, nor is the desire to become truly free ever extinguished.

This book rethinks a common definition of "Underground Railroad." It redefines Underground Railroad as "resistance to slavery through flight." This definition is more inclusive. It shifts attention to freedom seekers as central actors. It highlights the initiative of the freedom seekers. Freedom seekers share the limelight equally with their allies—the "conductors" and "station managers"—whose actions have long been celebrated. The history of freedom seekers takes on a new importance. The life stories of the book's subjects are more than adventures, local color or glimpses of a romantic past.

This book begins in Maryland, a small border state contributing more freedom seekers than its size would suggest. Located in the mid-Atlantic, it includes familiar Underground Railroad figures such as the Quakers because of the Quaker communities spread throughout the mid-Atlantic states. Highlighted whenever possible are the often-ignored African American participants in the Underground Railroad who gave refuge to and protected the freedom seekers.

Because of the state's proximity to Maryland, almost all the freedom seekers traveled through Pennsylvania and settled there at least temporarily. The exceptions, yet to be documented, might have been either those heading west following the National Road or the C&O Canal or those who used Maryland waterways to escape wherever they could. David Cecelski's book *The Waterman's Song: Slavery and Freedom in Maritime North Carolina* should have a counterpart looking at the role of the Chesapeake Bay in escapes from slavery.

The proposed definition of the Underground Railroad stretches to include where escapes started and finally ended, even if the eventual destination was across international borders. For this reason, the book is about Maryland—but not only about Maryland. Maryland is where the freedom seekers grew up in slavery, but in fear of slave catchers, they continued on through northern states, often to Canada and even the United Kingdom. They had to rebuild their lives far away from Maryland.

Slavery was not the only formative stage for the subjects of this book, although it marked their personalities for the rest of their lives. When freedom seekers took new names, this symbolized the beginning of their transformation into free people in the North or abroad. The story of their lives should extend into their maturity and reflect the extent to which they could be said to have achieved their goals for living in freedom.

This book gives a human face to history. It destroys stereotypes. It individualizes and concretizes the concept of the "freedom seeker." To make history more immediate and compelling, the book describes human emotions and aspirations. Its subjects each had their own personalities, talents, emotions, thoughts and motives. What sustained them were fear of the consequences of capture, a desire for freedom, a love of family and religious faith. It is striking to see the varied strategies these Marylanders chose and the varied types of networks they created in order to construct new lives.

Calling all the subjects "freedom seekers" should not imply that they shared the same dreams of freedom. At a minimum, however, the fleeing bondsmen all imagined liberty would allow them to earn a living wage; make their own decisions on residence, marriage and work; keep their families together; have religious freedom; and avoid physical abuse. By and large, these goals were attained. In addition, they each had their own expectations, which determined the ultimate degree of success they felt in their new lives. But, when pursuing personal dreams, the freedom seekers often had to revise their expectations when faced with prejudice, discrimination, restricted job opportunities and the inability to rise within the White world.

The book should serve as inspiration in Maryland, but not just Maryland. Heroes include people of all colors, ages and genders. All of this book's subjects and their allies were heroes for resisting the institution of slavery, regardless of the cost. They were realizing dreams of freedom and justice. Just a few can make a difference by maintaining hope for themselves and those left behind enslaved in whatever fashion. Those involved in the escape from slavery had the ability to transform their own lives and set an example for others. It was possible for freedom seekers to start and restart new lives multiple times, energized as they were by their hopes for a better life.

This book intends to make freedom seekers actors in the historical narrative of the pursuit of freedom, justice and full citizenship for all.

EPILOGUE

The story of the freedom seekers does not stop here. This book shows the importance of further research seeking the personalized information essential to understanding slavery and the Underground Railroad. Descendants of slaveholding families, as well as African American and Afro-Canadian descendants, still hold documentation privately, some shared and some not. Let us hope that those who have not shared can be persuaded. Access to private papers and oral traditions is essential to reconnect descendants of enslaved individuals with their own ancestral legacy and to give the general public a well-deserved understanding of the impact of the institution of slavery on individual Americans.

Appendix

MARYLAND NATIONAL UNDERGROUND RAILROAD NETWORK TO FREEDOM SITES, NATIONAL PARK SERVICE

Note: Sites not capitalized are private. Capitalized sites may be visited. Some are museums, but others have only a marker.

EASTERN SHORE SITES

Arthur Leverton's Farm Site
Preston, MD 21655
*No public access**

Belle Vue
Carmichael Road
Queenstown, MD 21658
*No public access**

BUTTON'S CREEK: JANE KANE ESCAPE SITE
MD Route 335 and Little Blackwater River
Church Creek, MD 21622

CAROLINE COUNTY COURTHOUSE AND JAIL
Courthouse Square
109 Market Street
Denton, MD 21629

Chesapeake and Delaware Canal (Museum)
815 Bethel Road
Chesapeake City, MD 21915

Choptank River
10215 River Landing Road
West Denton, MD 21629

Denton Steamboat Wharf
10219 River Landing Road
Denton, MD 21629

Dorchester County Courthouse
206 High Street
Cambridge, MD 21613

Grantham and Forrest Farm
31245 Chesterville Bridge Road
Millington, MD 21651
No public access*

Henry Highland Garnet Escape Site
MD 291, west of MD 290
Chesterville, MD 21620

Henry Massey Escape Site
142 Carriage Heath
Chester, MD 21619
No public access*

Isaac Henry Wright Farm Site
4042 Baker Road at Route 16
East New Market, MD 21613
No public access*

Jacob and Hannah Leverton House
3531 Seaman Road
Preston, MD 21655

Jacob Jackson Home Site
MD Route 16
Madison, MD 21648
*No public access**

JOSEPH CORNISH ESCAPE FROM GILPIN'S POINT
Holly Park Drive
Harmony, MD 21655

LIZZIE AMBY ESCAPE SITE/BAYLY HOUSE
207 High Street
Cambridge, MD 21612

LONG WHARF AT CAMBRIDGE
100 High Street
Cambridge, MD 21613

PARSON'S CREEK: KEENE FAMILY ESCAPE ROUTE
Parson's Creek at Route 16
Madison, MD 21648

PERRYVILLE RAILROAD FERRY AND STATION SITE
Perry Point VA Medical Center
Perry Point, MD 21902

POPLAR NECK PLANTATION AT MARSH CREEK
Northwest side of Marsh Creek Bridge
Poplar Neck Road
Preston, MD 21655.

Pritchett Meredith Farm
Bucktown and Decoursey Bridge Roads
Cambridge, MD 21613
*No public access**

REVEREND SAMUEL GREEN AND THE ORIGINAL COLORED PEOPLE'S
METHODIST EPISCOPAL CHURCH
509 Railroad Avenue
East New Market, MD 21631

Richard Potter Home Site
9 N. 4ᵗʰ Street
Denton, MD 21629

Richard Potter Rescue Celebration Site
4 N. 2ⁿᵈ Street
Denton, MD 21629

STAPLEFORT FARM: BOB MANOKEY
Wildlife Drive
Blackwater National Wildlife Refuge
2145 Key Wallace Drive
Cambridge, MD 21613

TURKEY POINT FARM, TURKEY POINT LIGHTHOUSE
4395 Turkey Point Road
North East, MD 21901

EASTERN SHORE PROGRAMS AND TOURS

A JOURNEY BEGINS: NATURE'S ROLE IN THE FLIGHT TO FREEDOM,
AN AUDIO TOUR
Adkins Arboretum
12610 Eveland Road
Ridgely, MD 21660

ADVENTURES OF HARRIET TUBMAN AND THE UNDERGROUND RAILROAD
AT BLACKWATER
2524 Key Wallace Drive
Cambridge, MD 21613

FREDERICK DOUGLASS DRIVING TOUR OF TALBOT COUNTY
11 S. Harrison Street
Easton, MD 21601

HARRIET TUBMAN ORGANIZATION TOURS
424 Race Street
Cambridge, MD 21613

HARRIET TUBMAN UNDERGROUND RAILROAD SCENIC BYWAY
Visitor Center at Sailwinds Park
2 Rose Hill Place
Cambridge, MD 21613

HARRIET TUBMAN UNDERGROUND RAILROAD VISITOR CENTER
4068 Golden Hill Road
Church Creek, MD 21622

WILLIAM STILL FAMILY INTERPRETIVE SITE
4-H Park
Detour Road
Denton, MD 21629

CENTRAL MARYLAND SITES

DUGAN'S WHARF
National Aquarium Pier 4
501 East Pratt Street
Baltimore, MD 21202

Eliza Howard Parker and Family Escape Site at Bellevue Farm
415 Oakington Road
Havre de Grace, MD 21078
*No public access**

ELKRIDGE FURNACE
5745 Furnace Avenue
Elkridge, MD 21075

Gorsuch Tavern
Verona, MD 21152
*No public access**

HAMPTON NATIONAL HISTORIC SITE
535 Hampton Lane
Towson, MD 21286

HAYS-HEIGHE HOUSE
401 Thomas Run Road
Bel Air, MD 21015

Howard County Courthouse 1843
8360 Court Avenue
Ellicott City, MD 21043
*No public access**

HOWARD COUNTY FIRST COURTHOUSE SITE
Ellicott Mills Drive at Main Street
Ellicott City, MD 21043

Howard County Jail
1 Emory Street
Ellicott City, MD 21043
*No public access**

MARYLAND STATE ARCHIVES
Hall of Records
350 Rowe Boulevard
Annapolis, MD 21401

MARYLAND STATE HOUSE
91 State Circle
Annapolis, MD 21401

MOUNT CLARE MUSEUM HOUSE
1500 Washington Boulevard
Baltimore, MD 21230

MOUNT CLARE STATION
901 W. Pratt Street
Baltimore, MD 21223

PRESIDENT STREET STATION/BALTIMORE CIVIL WAR MUSEUM
601 President Street
Baltimore, MD 21202

REDDY GRAY BURIAL SITE
Loudon Park National Cemetery
3445 Frederick Avenue
Baltimore, MD 21229

Roedown
3856 Wayson Road
Davidsonville, MD 21035
*No public access**

CENTRAL MARYLAND PROGRAMS AND TOURS

BANNEKER-DOUGLASS MUSEUM
84 Franklin Street
Annapolis, MD 21401

FREDERICK DOUGLASS FREEDOM AND HERITAGE TRAIL AND TOUR
PO Box 3014
Baltimore, MD 21229

HOWARD COUNTY HISTORICAL SOCIETY MUSEUM
8328 Court Avenue
Ellicott City, MD 21043

REGINALD F. LEWIS MUSEUM OF MARYLAND AFRICAN AMERICAN
HISTORY AND CULTURE
830 E. Pratt Street
Baltimore, MD 21202

SOUTHERN MARYLAND SITES

CAMP STANTON
South side of Route 231
Prince Frederick Road
Hughesville, MD 20637

JEFFERSON PATTERSON PARK AND MUSEUM
10515 Mackall Road
St. Leonard, MD 20685

OLD JAIL OF ST. MARY'S COUNTY
41625 Court House Drive
Leonardtown, MD 20650

POINT LOOKOUT STATE PARK & CIVIL WAR MUSEUM
11175 Point Lookout Road
Scotland, MD 20687

PORT TOBACCO COURTHOUSE
7215 Chapel Point Road
Port Tobacco, MD 20677

SOTTERLEY PLANTATION
44300 Sotterley Lane
Hollywood, MD 20636

CAPITAL REGION SITES

ARREST SITE OF WILLIAM CHAPLIN
Jesup Blair Local Park
900 Jesup Blair Road & Georgia Avenue
Silver Spring, MD 20912

BELAIR MANSION
12207 Tulip Grove Drive
Bowie, MD 20715

BERRY FARM AT OXON COVE PARK
6411 Oxon Hill Road
Oxon Hill, MD 20745

BEST FARM L'HERMITAGE
4801 Urbana Pike
Frederick, MD 21704

CATOCTIN IRON FURNACE AND MANOR HOUSE RUINS
Cunningham Falls State Park
Catoctin Furnace Road, Route 806
Thurmont, MD 21788

CHESAPEAKE AND OHIO CANAL
11710 MacArthur Boulevard
Potomac, MD 20854

DARNALL'S CHANCE HOUSE MUSEUM
14800 Governor Oden Bowie Drive
Upper Marlboro, MD 20772

ELIZABETH KECKLY BURIAL SITE
National Harmony Memorial Park
7101 Sheriff Road
Largo, MD 20792

JOSIAH HENSON MUSEUM AND PARK
11420 Old Georgetown Road
North Bethesda, MD 20852

MARIETTA HOUSE MUSEUM
5626 Bell Station
Glenn Dale, MD 20769

THE MOUNT CALVERT HISTORICAL & ARCHAEOLOGICAL PARK
16801 Mount Calvert Road
Upper Marlboro, MD 20772

MOUTH OF SWAN CREEK ESCAPE SITE
Fort Washington Park
13551 Fort Washington Road
Fort Washington, MD 20744

NORTHAMPTON SLAVE QUARTERS AND ARCHAEOLOGICAL PARK
10915 Water Port Court
Bowie, MD 20721

RIVERSDALE HOUSE MUSEUM
4811 Riverdale Road
Riverdale Park, MD 20737

Thornton Poole House
Glissans Mill Road
Linganore, MD 21771
No public access*

Capital Region Programs and Tours

In Their Steps: A Guided Walking Tour
29 Courthouse Square
Rockville, MD 20850

The Underground Railroad Experience in Maryland
Woodlawn Manor Cultural Park
16501 Norwood Road
Sandy Spring, MD 20860

Western Maryland Sites

Chesapeake and Ohio Canal
13 Canal St.
Cumberland, MD 21502

Ferry Hill Plantation
205 Potomac Street
Williamsport, MD 21795

Rockland
9030 Sharpsburg Pike
Fairplay, MD 21733
No public access*

NETWORK TO FREEDOM RESEARCH FACILITIES

Research facilities are places where you can learn more about the Underground Railroad through government documents, land records, fugitive slave records, census records, genealogy files and more.

HOWARD COUNTY HISTORICAL SOCIETY
9421 Frederick Road
Ellicott City, MD 21042

MARYLAND STATE ARCHIVES
350 Rowe Boulevard
Annapolis, MD 21401

MONTGOMERY HISTORY: JANE C. SWEEN RESEARCH LIBRARY AND SPECIAL COLLECTIONS
42 West Middle Lane
Rockville, MD 20850

SOUTHERN MARYLAND STUDIES CENTER
College of Southern Maryland Library Building
Room LR211
8730 Mitchell Road
La Plata, MD 20646

TODD RESEARCH CENTER
Dorchester County Historical Society
1003 Greenway Drive
Cambridge, MD 21613

SELECTED SOURCES

Evidence of escapes from Maryland is found in archival records housed in the state's archival repositories, universities, historical societies and private family collections. Some government records, like court cases and probate records, are still held in local county offices, such as the county courts or registers of wills, or have been donated to local historical societies by individuals whose ancestors privately retained this public information.

The Maryland State Archives is the state's central repository for state government records of permanent value and has documents on incidents of flight, assistance to flight and flight prevention. The archives has extracted important information and made it available on a website called "The Legacy of Slavery in Maryland." Some clearly identifiable records that showcase relevant incidents are the Runaway Docket and the Maryland Penitentiary Records. Regular correspondence in Governor Proceedings includes that between governors seeking to have individuals identified as runaways extradited to their home state. For example, the governor of Maryland might write to the governor of Pennsylvania requesting the return of an enslaved person or might receive a request for the return of an enslaved person believed to be hiding within the borders of Maryland. It is important to note that numerous other records may be overlooked because they are filed in a way not suggesting Underground Railroad activity.

Another resource that documents enslaved communities in Maryland is the 1850 and 1860 Federal Slave Schedules, part of United States Census records. The schedules list owners by name, with listings of unnamed enslaved individuals represented by gender, skin color and age. The schedules also list the number of slave cabins on a particular property. Most importantly, the schedules count the individuals identified as runaways.

Maryland university archives and research centers have private records. The University of Maryland digital library has documents on its website that highlight runaway slaves, including broadsides from Frederick County and Prince George's County, a statement of complaint against a sheriff for allowing an enslaved man to run at large and escape and an account book of enslaved people to be sold by a member of a renowned slaveholding family, Charles Benedict Calvert. There are additional offerings on Digital Maryland, a web-based platform that collaboratively makes accessible records from the holdings of organizations including but not limited to the Enoch Pratt Library in Baltimore, Prince George's County Historical Society and the University of Maryland–Baltimore County. The *Baltimore Sun*, the major Maryland newspaper in the antebellum era, is available and searchable in digitized form.

The following websites are useful:
Digital Maryland: https://www.digitalmaryland.org
Documenting the American South: https://www.docsouth.unc.edu
Maryland State Archives: https://www.msa.md.gov
Maryland State Archives Legacy of Slavery: http://slavery.msa.maryland.gov

Introduction

Alpert, Jonathan. "The Origin of Slavery in the United States—The Maryland Precedent." *American Journal of Legal History* 14, no. 3 (July 1970), 189–221.

Bancroft, Frederic. *Slave Trading in the Old South*. Columbia: University of South Carolina Press, 1996. Originally published 1931.

Blackett, R.J.M. *The Captive's Quest for Freedom: Fugitive Slaves, the 1850 Fugitive Slave Law, and the Politics of Slavery*. Cambridge, UK: Cambridge University Press, 2018.

Blassingame, John W., ed. *Slave Testimony: Two Centuries of Letters, Speeches, Interviews, and Autobiographies*. Baton Rouge: Louisiana State University Press, 1977.

Blight, David W. *Frederick Douglass: Prophet of Freedom*. New York: Simon & Schuster, 2018.

Delbanco, Andrew. *The War before the War: Fugitive Slaves and the Struggle for America's Soul from the Revolution to the Civil War*. New York: Penguin, 2018.

Diggins, Milt. *Stealing Freedom along the Mason-Dixon Line: Thomas McCreary, the Notorious Slave Catcher from Maryland*. Baltimore: Maryland Historical Society, 2015.

Fields, Barbara Jeanne. *Slavery and Freedom in the Middle Ground: Maryland during the Nineteenth Century*. New Haven, CT: Yale University Press, 1985.

Franklin, John Hope, and Loren Schweninger. *Runaway Slaves: Rebels on the Plantation*. New York: Oxford University Press, 1999.

Jones, Martha S. *Birthright Citizens: A History of Race and Rights in Antebellum America*. Cambridge, UK: Cambridge University Press, 2018.

Larson, Kate. *Bound for the Promised Land: Harriet Tubman, Portrait of an American Hero*. New York: Ballantine Books, 2004.

Ricks, Mary Kay. *Escape on the Pearl: Heroic Bid for Freedom on the Underground Railroad*. New York: William Morrow, 2007.

Sinha, Manisha. *The Slave's Cause: A History of Abolition*. New Haven, CT: Yale University Press, 2016.

Smith, Gene Allen. *The Slaves' Gamble: Choosing Sides in the War of 1812*. New York: Palgrave MacMillan, 2013.

Thomas, William G., III. *A Question of Freedom: The Families Who Challenged Slavery from the Nation's Founding to the Civil War*. New Haven, CT: Yale University Press, 2020.

Alexander Helmsley

Drew, Benjamin. *A North-Side View of Slavery. The Refugee: or the Narratives of Fugitive Slaves in Canada*. Boston: John Jewett, 1856.

Finkelman, Paul. "Chief Justice Hornblower of New Jersey and the Fugitive Slave Law of 1793." In *Slavery and the Law*, ed. Paul Finkelman. Madison, WI: Madison House, 1996.

Friend. "Upholding Slavery." Vol. 9, no. 36 (June 11, 1836): 281–82.

Gigantino, James J., II. *The Ragged Road to Abolition: Slavery and Freedom in New Jersey, 1775–1865*. Philadelphia: University of Pennsylvania Press, 2015.

Still, William. *The Underground Railroad*. Chicago: Ebony Classics, Johnson Publishing, 1970. Originally published 1871.

Moses Viney

Concordiensis. "Moses Viney." Vol. 32, no 9, published by Union College (January 15, 1908).

Hathaway, Gretchel. *A Bonded Friendship: Moses and Eliphalet*. New York: Lexingford, 2016.

S., H.A. "Moses Viney." *Garnet* (1910): 277–84.

W., W.L. "Moses." *Garnet* (1896): 207–8.

Wright, A.S. "Moses." *Concordiensis* 18, no. 9, Union College (February 13, 1895).

Yetwin, Neil B. "The Odyssey of Moses Viney, parts 1-6." *Schenectady County Historical Society Newsletter* (vol. 37, nos. 9–10, May–June 2001, through vol. 39, nos. 3–4, March–April 2002).

Basil Dorsey

Bacon, Margaret Hope. *But One Race: The Life of Robert Purvis.* Albany: State University of New York Press, 2007.

Hampshire Gazette (Northampton, MA). "Basil Dorsey." April 2, 1867.

Magill, Edward H. "When Men Were Sold: The Underground Railroad in Bucks County." *Bucks Intelligencer*, March 31, 1898.

Smedley, R.C. *History of the Underground Railroad in Chester and the Neighboring Counties of Pennsylvania.* Mechanicsburg, PA: Stackpole Books, 2005. Originally published in 1883.

Strimer, Steve. "Basil Dorsey: Basil Dorsey Escapes from Liberty, Maryland Plantation to Settle in Florence." Freedom Stories of the Pioneer Valley. http://freedomstoriespv.wordpress.com.

W.H.J. "(From the National Inquirer) Slave Case in Bucks County." *Colored American* (New York, NY), September 2, 1837.

John Thompson

Bolster, W. Jeffrey. *Black Jacks: African American Seamen in the Age of Sail.* Cambridge, MA: Harvard University Press, 1997.

Grover, Kathryn. *Fugitive's Gibraltar: Escaping Slaves and Abolitionism in New Bedford, Massachusetts.* Amherst: University of Massachusetts, 2001.

McCarthy, B. Eugene, and Thomas L. Doughton, eds. *From Bondage to Belonging: The Worcester Slave Narratives.* Amherst: University of Massachusetts, 2007.

Thompson, John. *The Life of John Thompson, a Fugitive Slave.* Ed. William L. Andrews. New York: Penguin, 2011. Originally published in 1856.

James Watkins

Beeching, Barbara. *Hopes and Expectations: The Origins of the Black Middle Class in Hartford.* Albany: State University of New York Press, 2017.

Blackett, R.J.M. *Building an Antislavery Wall: Black Americans in the Atlantic Abolitionist Movement, 1830–1860.* Ithaca: Cornell University Press, 1983.

Frederick Douglass Paper (Rochester, NY). "Escaped Slaves from the 'Land of Freedom.'" November 8, 1853. (Copied from *Birmingham Mercury*.)

———. "To the Editor of *Aris's Gazette.*" June 16, 1853.

———. "American Slavery." January 29, 1852. (Copied from *Bolton Chronicle*.)

Murray, Hannah-Rose. *Advocates of Freedom: African American Transatlantic Abolitionism in the British Isles.* Cambridge, UK: Cambridge University Press, 2020.

Watkins, James. *Narrative of the Life of James Watkins.* Dodo Press: n.d., n.p.

Webber, Christopher L. *American to the Backbone: The Life of James W.C. Pennington, the Fugitive Slave Who Became One of the First Black Abolitionists.* New York: Pegasus, 2011.

Matilda and Richard Neal

Anti-Slavery Bugle (New Lisbon, OH). "Kidnapping." February 5, 1853.

Baltimore (MD) Sun. "The Arrest in Philadelphia." January 28, 1853.

Morris, Anthony. *The Abduction of Richard Neal: A Story Seldom Told*. West Conshohocken, PA: Infinity Press, 2015.

National Anti-Slavery Standard (New York, NY, and Philadelphia, PA). "A Shameful Outrage." February 10, 1853.

Isaac Mason

Greenwood, Janette Thomas. *First Fruits of Freedom: The Migration of Former Slaves and Their Search for Equality in Worcester, Massachusetts, 1862–1900*. Chapel Hill: University of North Carolina Press, 2009.

McCarthy, B. Eugene, and Thomas L. Doughton, eds. *From Bondage to Belonging: The Worcester Slave Narratives*. Amherst: University of Massachusetts Press, 2007.

Salvatore, Nick. *We All Got History: The Memory Books of Amos Webber*. Urbana: University of Illinois Press, 1996.

Standard Union (Brooklyn, NY). "The Tribute of Senator Hoar." September 2, 1898.

Worcester (MA) Telegram. "Born in Slavery, Dies a Leader." August 27, 1898.

———. "Isaac Mason's Celebration." May 15, 1897.

Hester Norman

Baltimore (MD) Sun. "Slave and Riot Case." August 30, 1847; August 31, 1847; September 1, 1847.

Carlisle (PA) Herald. "Tumult and Riot." June 9, 1847. House Divided: The Civil War Research Engine at Dickinson College. http://housedivided.dickinson.edu/ugrr/news_june1847.html.

Coval, Jennifer. "Bound for Freedom: Eastern State Penitentiary and the Eleven Convicted 'Rioters' in the Carlisle Fugitive Slave Riot of 1847." Unpublished paper in files of Eastern State Penitentiary Historic Site, Philadelphia, PA.

Crooks, George R. *Life and Letters of the Rev. John McClintock*. New York: Nelson & Phillips, 1876.

Slotten, Martha C. "The McClintock Slave Riot of 1847." *Carlisle County History* 17, no. 1 (2000): 14–35.

Smith, David G. *On the Edge of Freedom: The Fugitive Slave Issue in South Central Pennsylvania, 1820–1870*. New York: Fordham University Press, 2013.

Wingert, Cooper H. *Abolitionists of South Central Pennsylvania*. Charleston, SC: The History Press, 2018.

James Hamlet

Foner, Eric. *Gateway to Freedom: The Hidden History of the Underground Railroad*. New York: Norton, 2015.

North Star (Rochester, NY). "First Case Under the Fugitive Slave Law." October 3, 1850.

Papenfuse, Edward C. "'History from the Bottom Up:' Clementina Grierson Rind (1740?–1774) & James Hamlet (1822–?)." February 2020. http://www.rememberingbaltimore.net/.

Papson, Don, and Tom Calarco. *Secret Lives of the Underground Railroad in New York City: Sydney Howard Gay, Louis Napoleon and the Record of Fugitives*. Jefferson, NC: McFarland, 2015.

[Lewis Tappan]. *The Fugitive Slave Bill: Its History and Unconstitutionality: With an Account of the Seizure and Enslavement of James Hamlet, and His Subsequent Restoration to Liberty*. New York: William Harned, 1850.

INDEX

W

Z

ABOUT THE AUTHOR

Corinne Masur.

Jenny Masur is a native Washingtonian. She worked for seventeen years for the National Park Service as National Capital Regional Manager for the National Underground Railroad Network to Freedom. Her doctorate is in anthropology, and her interest in individual lives dates from the oral history she coedited while in graduate school. Her respect for the heroes of the Underground Railroad continues to grow.

Visit us at
www.historypress.com